POLARIZED

a bipolar memoir

By

Patricia Frisch, Ph.D.

Patricia Frisch

This book was provided by our lending library. Please don't let it gather dust on your book shelf! Pass it on or return to us at:
NAMI Austin P.O Box 302398
Austin, TX 78703
512-420-9810
www.namiaustin.org

email: polarizedmemoir@gmail.com

website: www.patriciafrischphd.com

VIP business profile: www.worldwidewhoswho.com

Copyright © 2012 by Patricia Frisch, Ph.D.
All rights reserved.

ISBN: 1-4679-6629-0
ISBN-13: 978-1-4679-6629-0

FOR RICHARD

In thankfulness for his love, kindness, and support,
during forty-three years of marriage.
May God grant us many more years together.

TABLE OF CONTENTS

Author's Notes i

Preface iii

Chapter One 1

Chapter Two 21

Chapter Three 33

Chapter Four 55

Chapter Five 67

Chapter Six 83

Chapter Seven 107

Chapter Eight 123

Chapter Nine 137

AUTHOR'S NOTES

The names of most people and places used in this memoir are changed to fictitious names or references such as brother, aunt and so forth for privacy. The few exceptions are family and friends who wished to be mentioned: Richard, my husband; Kathleen, my sister; and Margo Berk, my life-long friend. Emphasis in this memoir is based on sharing with the readers how I coped with bipolar 1 disorder and led a good life despite the disorder. Therefore, I did not write about my children. I suffice it to say that they are leading their own healthy adult lives. It is not a book about my family. As parents, Richard and I taught them the same self-care that we used in our own lives. For anonymity, all places are eliminated except the Empire State building in New York City.

PREFACE

I wrote a memoir because it is a slice of my life, narrower in scope than an autobiography or biography. The latter draw on fuller accounts of an individual's life and relationships. I decided to report painful components of my bipolar 1 disorder mainly to have a basis for sharing the unique material that helped me to live with bipolarity and enjoy life. The memoir doesn't cover one time in my life. It runs the gamut from individual, child, adolescent, wife, mother, teacher, counselor, student, friend and colleague.

In my childhood, I never complained about the physical pain when the disorder was manifest; so my parents did not undertand my disorder. Researchers may be interested in my early childhood and adolescent distorted thinking and behaving. I fared better once I was in the stimulating environment of college. However, my momentum picked up measurably later on when I had proper medical attention. As I became a young adult, the full force of anxiety and depression was similar to a tornado, but commonly referred to as a breakdown. In a hospital at twenty-six, I finally received medication. It is probably the most significant of the building blocks for coping with bipolar disorder. I began to build a new life for myself that I had never experienced before. I share all I can think of that helped me from that point until the present.

Individuals have written to help people understand mental illness or the effect on family life. I have chosen to write about myself in the hopes that my positive approaches and ideas in life will be available and valuable to others. I hope the readers, especially researchers or clinicians, those who have suffered mental illness, perhaps have a family member or friend with the disease, or an interest in further education about bipolarity, will feel free to pick my memoir apart for imaginative insights, skills, and motivation. Leave the rest behind.

CHAPTER ONE

Childhood (1955-1962)

When I was a six-year old girl, I stood on the observation deck of the Empire State Building in New York City. I was getting ready to jump. My little life pulsed in rapidly beating measures. Each moment moved me another step closer to a dramatic ending. I had composed a plan to end the awful pains that I felt inside of my body and mind. I believed that I was almost on the brink of relief.

Daddy drove on family outings. Mom, my brother, and my sister and I were treated to long and pleasant countryside drives or a special sightseeing place to explore.

These trips were part and parcel of daddy's agenda for being a parent. He always believed in education for his children. Those Sunday afternoons were educational trips for his family. During the week he would drive us to school before he caught the train to work.

"Go inside now and get an itch-ucation!" He would laugh while his wavy black hair would jiggle. His Irish face and very blue eyes would crinkle. He was a Navy officer during World War II, a well-educated individual with an electrical engineering B.S. from NYU. He was also a scholar who could read Greek and Latin. He loved to debate with his friends on any topic, especially with Norman Berk, a psychologist and good friend.

Norman, a young Jewish man would be safe to stay home during World War II. He had just finished his Masters of Psychology (M.A.) from the

University of Illinois. He was accepted to an M.D. program, but had to wait because the Jewish quota was filled. However, he joined the Air Force to help stop Hitler. When he returned to New York, he married Eileen Grabson and he entered a Ph.D. program in psychology at NYU. The Berk family was to be an integral part of our lives as we went forward together.

My mom was a slight, very bright woman, a natural red head with beautiful blue eyes. She gave up her career on Wall Street on daddy's insistence when she became pregnant. I do not think she was very happy about his viewpoint. Today she would have had a career and raised us. She loved the challenges of her work like any contemporary woman. She worked diligently with us at home and was enthusiastic about our family outings. Around the house she often had a preoccupied look on her face, as if she were remembering her exciting days on Wall Street. The trips were an intriguing change of pace for mom.

I started to feel queasy and uncomfortable during the family outings. I was only six years old; I did not have the vocabulary to explain feeling guilty or anxious. Awful captures the feeling of too much pain in my arms, legs, and head, to sit still in the car. I was told that I was misbehaving. I wished to be happy like the rest of the family, so I taught myself to hold the pain in, squeeze it hard, and smile. I was happy to belong and have a special trip, but the price was getting pretty heavy to tolerate. Because daddy was very strict I never uttered a peep about the way I felt. I continued to hold my anxious feelings close inside. It never occurred to me that telling mom or daddy that I wanted to cry out from the pain would help. As a family we tended to be stoics. Daddy, like many Irish descendants, was an authoritarian man - a gentleman of one-way conversations.

Saturday afternoons would find him with his cronies at one of our small local bars for a few brews. His fairly large stomach and generally pudgy frame belied his alternative stress reducer: food, especially large steaks and corn on the cob with lots of butter. Medical education was not readily available as it is today.

Family outings are usually fun-filled chances for bonding with one another. Mine were quite different, to say the least. On one Sunday ride, I was asked to sit in the front seat of our Buick Roadmaster. Most children would enjoy being singled out by their parents. Suffocated, trapped feelings flashed inside of me like bright lights. When I shut my eyes they alternated bright white and yellow. The prickly sensations in my torso, arms, legs, head and face, I now know as a severe anxiety. Squeezed between my parents, I became a fossil like impression in the car seat. (A fossil is formed between two rocks or in the crevice of a rock. Children or adults alike enjoy cracking them open with a hammer to see animal impressions). I thought that being near the parents caused these feelings. Brash lights exploded in my mind every time either parent moved, touched, or squished me, without realizing the pain it caused. Snow like clouds covered my inner landscape as tingling pain shot all over my limbs. I longed for some kind of oblivion that would end the dreaded episodes on our family trips.

I finally decided that I would not be able to take a car ride like the last one ever again. Aches of blinding terror combined with jarring lights and bumpy roads suggested the need for a new destination. I sat still so that daddy could drive the car. I spent my front seat time looking for a way out of the car and the bad feelings. Short of an answer, endurance was becoming my giftedness.

During a weeknight meal, mom and daddy told us about the wonderful plans they had made for our next trip. Immediately, bright lights crept into my mind behind closed eyes.

"Why aren't you paying attention?" my daddy asked me in his severe authoritarian tone of voice.

"I was thinking hard so I had to close my eyes," I said. It was true. I was thinking about how to escape this next trip.

Mom continued in a happy tone of voice that was easy for her to acquire. I dimly remember not being able to parrot her pleasant words because it seemed too difficult. She told us that we would be going to the Empire State

Building in New York City. We would have an exciting adventure. We would go all of the way to the top of the tallest building in New York City in an elevator. It was a magnificent elevator that could somehow manage to carry us to the ninety-ninth floor. Up on the top was an observation deck. We would be able to see all the buildings and waterways around the island of Manhattan. The sky would be above us and the lake in Central Park would be beneath us.

When I heard about this last jaunt, it truly sounded like the escape that I needed. I was starting to worry how I was going to stop the foggy inner vision and blazing lights rotating around behind my closed eyes. Nobody could see the pain building in my mind until I was ready to burst. My head felt blown up like a birthday balloon bobbing around without any of the fun.

I said nothing to my parents about the strange pains. My mom used to tell us the story about my sister, Kathleen, skinning her knee. Flesh was hanging off and blood was dripping profusely from the wound. She simply walked over to mom and showed her what happened. She had no tears or screams. I never heard my parents arguing. Daddy would raise his voice and his face would turn red when angry about something we did, but he never spanked us.

I decided that the observation deck of the Empire State building was the place to hatch my plan to rid myself of the pain. The elevator would travel rapidly to the top so I had no chance to change my mind. I could picture myself getting off the elevator. I could look down upon the lake in Central Park.

I would jump.

In my imagination I saw the feelings fall away before I landed. At the age of six, suicide was a term belonging to an inaccessible adult world. All I thought that I was going to do was end the nightmarish pain in my mind and body. Loving my family, hating the feelings generated around them, I was very confused; I wanted escape from the alarming lights, fog, and the tingling in my limbs. My vivid imagination only had plans to leave the anxious realities behind. Like an artist's mind, I could only approximate the picture awaiting me on the canvas. During the family outing, the brushstroke of a protective community was yet to stop my dysfunctional plans.

I remember very little of the preparations earlier in that day for the outing. My memory goes back as far as the elevator ride. As my family rose, we could hear the noise of the gears screeching in the elevator shaft. The panel lights blinked as we traveled the ninety-nine floors. I felt closed in, excited, and frightened. My parents held onto the walls of the elevator as it rose to the observation tower. My sister and brother also looked just as concerned about the safely of the slow rising elevator. We exited near the top on the observation deck. We gave a collective sigh of relief to be out of the lights and closeness in the elevator cage. I was secretly thrilled to be where it was high enough for my jump.

Before entering the observation deck, daddy needed to purchase tickets. It was October and my birthday was right around the corner. He was looking in a display case of jewelry next to the ticket booth. The bracelets had a charm on a gold chain. The charm had a globe of the whole world and a colored opal like stone in the middle. My delusions told me that daddy would be there when I returned after the jump. For now, he asked me if I would like a bracelet. I have the memories of the whole world turning in circles as he placed that bracelet on my arm and clasped it tight. My unspoken awareness was that it would be nice to wear for the jump.

I smiled up at my daddy. The gift was about life to him, and to me, freedom from all that would not allow me to cry out. It was a gift for October birthday girls. My foggy mind continued to cover and overwhelm all other factors of the family trip. The bangle bracelet swayed on my wrist as I would soon sway in the breeze all by myself.

At last I walked onto the deck once seen in my parents' travel brochures. Out of the corner of my mind, I spotted a guard (for people like me). I can still remember his presence piercing the throbbing in my chest and arms. He was overwhelming my plans. His official garb – complete with a litany of badges and patches – stopped my escape mode.

Then the family walked over to the edge. I remember looking down as if I was all by myself. Surprisingly thick, high, and pointed black iron bars curled inward toward me and away from the huge sky. I went over to the side of the deck and felt the bars. I peered through them. Just as mom had told us, I could see the lake in Central Park. I saw the endpoint of my goal to escape those feelings that happened to me on these family trips.

For most of my life, even during grandiose or suicide thoughts, I could close my eyes and imagine those black bars in my imagination. I could see the bars inside my hands, where I could grasp and use them. I met these boundaries that day, and they became similar to life long friends. They helped me stop short of all kinds of harm.

The boundaries of my bracelet, the guard, and the bars touched my congealing fear thoroughly enough to produce rational thoughts. My daddy or the guard might stop me. Or the guard might turn me over to daddy. I might not get through the bars. The survival thoughts were increasing in speed. Daddy would be furious with me.

He had never spanked me, but who knows? Only once had he threatened me with a belt. My greater concern was that he might confine me to solitude in my bedroom where my trapped feelings were severe. The bars, the guard, and my daddy had foiled my plans.

My goal was sidetracked. Any day of the week, I can see the lake and the bars in my imagination. Yet I have no childhood recollection of dwelling upon the observation deck after that day. Sequestered somewhere in the corners of my mind, my childhood as a six year old continued with focus on present time activities. The lake, bars, guard, and bracelet remain parts of my journey through mental illness as an adult. They are pieces of darkness that have a redeeming quality. They have supported my efforts to stay away from whatever does not work for me. They still worked in the chaos of my mind. Long before I encountered psychotherapy or medicine, they are memorial to my experience of limits and boundaries. I learned a lot one harrowing day on the observation tower.

For the rest of my life there were to be limits and boundaries that would pop out as the lesson plans of my life that I may have otherwise thrown away. Anytime I was in New York City and I had the courage to look up to the Empire State Building observation deck, I was reminded that along with doctors, medicine, and therapy, I had once recognized the self-empowerment that comes from paying attention to caring people in the community. I felt limited by the love in my daddy's eyes when he snapped on the bracelet. The boundaries limited my potential self-destructive habits such as a jumping through the air to death in the lake in Central Park. Relief came as the pressure in my head and body began to subside.

The next morning after the thwarted attempt, I was awakened by my mom's cheerful voice and a cold cloth applied to my sleepy eyes. She did her washcloth extra after a long day of family outings because Kathleen and I were hard to rouse for school the next day. This gesture was always mom's way of gently waking us up for school ever since kindergarten. It was so much nicer than being yelled at that it was time to start a new day. The texture of the cloth was just a little rough, and its coolness awakened me without startling me. Mom always disciplined us in the most peaceful ways possible.

The emotional pain of my childhood would disappear as quickly as it had started. Like throwing a sharp and clear switch, my attention was on going to school the next morning. Yesterday did not enter into today. The wonderful childhood adventures that every young person deserves were once again my reality.

Summertime was my favorite time of the year. My inner lights were exchanged for the beautiful stars at night, coupled with sunshine by day.

Walking around in my front yard, I can remember thanking God for everything. I would beg God to extend my life at home as long as possible before I had to grow up. The smell of grass cut by push lawn mowers whirling on Saturday mornings, the fragrance of lilies of the valley bobbing their tiny white heads alongside the next-door-neighbors' driveway, and cherry blossoms blooming outside an upstairs window beckoned to my imagination.

Cherries on the tree outside an upstairs bedroom were for picking, bagging, and selling to the neighbors from a little wagon. When gathering the succulent cherries, we secured ourselves on sturdy branches to pick, pick, pick. Kathleen and her friend would pull a wagon from house to house with their juicy wares. Other days Kathleen and I would play all day long in the cherry, maple, dogwood, and apple trees in our yard. Mom would hand ham and cheese sandwiches up through the leaves and blossoms. On the days when we finished with our wonderful cherry-picking task, we would continue to play house in the branches until dusk.

When all the cherries were gone, we would turn to designing neighborhood fairs and talent shows. I was usually the organizer. Talent shows happened across the street in a friend's backyard tool shed. Tap dancing, ballet, and accordion playing were the backbone of these afternoons with no admission fee. Kathleen and I sported costumes from our dance recitals. One summer we spent many days painting pictures and inviting the parents to come to an art exhibit called, "A Penny for Your Thoughts". Each abstract piece of art we created had a jar next to it; the adults were to place their best guess about each of the children's paintings in the jar. The adult with the most imaginative answer won a penny. One backyard fair yielded $6.78 that we designated for the children in the hospital down the street. At the end of the day we all walked together to the hospital office and handed in the envelope. We were really proud of our gift.

Some summer days in the late afternoon, my mom, Kathleen, and I would end the day at one of the town's rocky beaches. Late afternoon sun was easier on our fair Irish complexions. To walk on the rocky beaches called for a ritual preparation starting in the springtime. We would take off our shoes and walk barefoot everyday after school to prepare our feet for the rocky beaches. It toughened the soles of our feet and provided a natural excitement. For it was springtime, almost summertime, and almost the end of the year at the Catholic school we attended in town.

Winter sometimes brought the fun of snow that heralds sled riding. One snowy Sunday afternoon my parents wanted to take us on another outing. I did not want to go. My parents decided that it would be okay for me to stay at home. The only rule was that I did not go sled riding in the gully with the older kids. I was only eight or nine. The gully was around the corner and down three blocks of suburban homes.

I waved good-bye to my parents. After the car pulled out of sight, I felt a blurry relief because I had avoided the anxiety associated with a family trip. I walked to the garage in my new rubber boots that were under the Christmas tree a few weeks ago.

I wiped off my Speedway sled, left the garage, and skipped through the snow. I passed neighbors cleaning snow off of their bushes. They waived their brooms at me. Smiling, I waved back to them. The exhilaration of nature ran through my bones as I continued to speed toward the gully. I did not think anything could happen. The sky held a muted haze. I only thought about being with the older kids. Watching how they jumped on their sleds, I could imitate their swift and superior moves.

When I got to the woods, the older kids readily included me in the fun. Standing in line, it was finally my turn to whiz down the hill. A boy at the end of the icy run stood in front of a large tree. He dropped his hand to signal that it was my turn to come down. I shot my exhilarated energy over the beginning ledge, bumping over sticks, twigs, and roots under the ice and snow. The run was more difficult than I had anticipated. In my emotional excitement I did not observe a crucial maneuver. Each kid twisted his or her sled to the left to avoid the tree. I was not thinking as I came to the end of the run, and so I slammed into the tree. The boy managing the runs jumped aside to avoid being hit. I heard a crunch as my forehead hit the bottom of the tree. I got up and walked through the woods alone. The older kids were too busy sledding to notice me.

After my accident, the only thing left for me to do was drag my sled home. Putting my hand on my forehead, I could feel the right side beginning to swell. When I arrived home and put my sled away in the garage, all I could think of doing was combing my bangs over my forehead. If my parents saw my forehead, I was going to be in hot water. At dinner, I sat down with plastered bangs. Mom looked curiously at me.

"Patricia, how come you have your bangs pasted down on your forehead? You don't usually wear your hair that way.

"Brush them aside, please," she demanded.

Mom and dad saw the bump. I had to explain. The truth might cancel the punishment for my disobedience. I was sent to my room soon after the explanation was out of my mouth. I was finished in more ways than one. I imagine that my mom sent me to my room with an ice pack, but I don't remember. No memory is necessary as I still have a bump to remind me of my escapade. The uncomfortable, queasy feelings were worse when I realized that I now had some real sins for confession to the priest on Saturday down at our Catholic church.

Movement such as dance was soothing to me. In retrospect, it helped my ruffled emotions. When I aligned my behavior with adult expectations it only came at the great price of anxiety that dance alleviated. I started taking dancing lessons, ballet and tap, at a local studio when I was nine years old. By the time I was ten, the owner had asked me to become a paid assistant teacher. $1.00 per hour was a lot of money in those days. I wondered if she was being kind or if I was talented. Such insecure questions always haunted me. Mutuality of needs and wants was a difficult concept for me to grasp with a mind that was becoming rigid, easily preoccupied, and scrupulous from guilt, with a severe drop in self-esteem. However, these thoughts blocked even greater pain from emerging.

One Saturday the family raked leaves into huge piles for daddy to burn. Mom called me in to set the lunch table. I learned in school that the people in France set the table for left-handed people so that they could crossover when picking up their forks like right-handed people. Being left-landed, I thought this idea was an exciting adventure. Although not French, I would belong to a group just like everyone else belonged somewhere.

Daddy came into the dining room, took one look at my handiwork, and sent me to my bedroom for setting the table incorrectly. I managed insistent cries of protest based on school information, but he didn't listen. Apparently all of those educational outings didn't include my observations of life. I ran upstairs crying until called down for lunch, where I picked up the correctly placed fork in front of me with my left hand. Once again, I was different but not in a clever French way. Daddy had told mom that I was more sensitive than my brother or sister; they had to be on guard because of my obvious differences. I was never aware of what they did and if they knew what to do.

After that lunch I'd show my denial of daddy's existence and lack of interest when he came home from a trip. Once I sat next to him in the living room and did not say hello or run to him.

"Daddy, welcome home!" was less often my standard greeting. He gave me a pencil as a little gift from his trip in upstate NY.

"Thank you," I said. However, my face showed the awkwardness of being around him once again. Sitting in the living room, he gave me the pencil.

"I remembered you but you did not remember me while I was away," he said. I felt guilty that I really didn't want to see him anymore. The emotional turmoil was too hard.

One night I knelt down and prayed for him not to come home. I had not intended to kill him with my prayers, but my guilt and anxiety mounted beyond anything I had ever imagined a human being could feel.

When asked about my parents by every therapist in my adult life, I would always mention that my father died when I was ten years old. I was the one who answered the phone the night daddy died. We had what is now called a landline that sat on a small, not too sturdy wooden table in the hallway of our Cape Cod style home. It was right across from the Fibber McGee closet where my mother kept her ironing and junk that she would never throw out. The phone rang and I picked it up.

"Hello, Patricia, get mom for me," Daddy said. After mom spoke to him, she put the phone down, and immediately asked my brother to take her to the hospital in New York City. Kathleen and I spent the night with close friends.

Mom would always tell her friends what a wonderful job my brother did of maneuvering in and out of the New York traffic at rush hour to get to the hospital. My brother got her to the hospital in time to see daddy. The doctor explained that daddy had had another heart attack. Later, a priest came into the room and wanted mom to leave so he could hear daddy's confession. She was waiting in the hall when the priest came out.

"I'm afraid your husband has died," he said to mom. Mom never completed the mourning process. Years later at the age of ninety-one, she still became emotional looking back at the night daddy died.

"He hadn't done anything wrong. He didn't need confession," she said crying and squealing. A peace settled over her after releasing her hurt feelings that day at ninety-one.

The day after daddy died, my mom and my brother picked us up from our close friends' home. Their mom knew daddy had died. She sensitively didn't tell us because mom was about to do that very difficult task on the way home. My brother was driving the car and she turned to us in the back seat. Kathleen looked stunned. I was able to cry a little bit. When we arrived at home, the house was full of people cooking, bringing baked goods, and mostly putting things away in the wrong places while they laughed. My uncle scooped me up, crying, in his lap. He told me that my daddy was in heaven. After the funeral, this uncle came every Thanksgiving and Christmas and some weekends in between. He was a most welcome guest who had loved my daddy, the youngest of six children.

We were allowed to see my daddy at the funeral parlor. He looked pretty okay to me. The funeral was in the little Catholic church I loved. The casket was up front and we sat next to it. During the recessional I remember seeing my cousin crying. I remember little else. We were not to go to the gravesite. My aunt, who visited us for a few days, laughing and weeping with my mom, took us to a diner for breakfast. Sitting next to Kathleen, she wrapped her full taffeta skirt around Kathleen, making her feel comfortable. Months later, my mom took us to our father's gravesite in a military graveyard. She's next to him now.

When my daddy was alive he was instrumental in having a park closed near our home opened once again. He was in the newspaper. The park had baseball fields where my brother liked to play, streams for sailing little boats that children would run and catch, a skating pond in the winter, swings, slides, and picnic tables. People would bring blankets and listen to concerts in front of the museum. Many a day I would sit in the park by the lake and cry. I did some of my mourning in the loveliest of settings my daddy left behind for all to enjoy.

The mourning process was difficult for all of us. It was especially hard on my mother. My grandmother lived with us and she died in March of 1959. My father died in July of the same year. Two months later my brother went off to college. Our neighbor across the street took Kathleen, my brother, my mother, and me to the airport. I can still remember my mom standing on the observation deck. To add to her sadness she had twisted her ankle and had a cast on her foot. I can still remember her arching and stretching up and looking toward the plane as her only son flew away to his own adulthood.

Many forms of therapeutic intervention were not available when my daddy died. Grief work was unheard of. However, mom searched around for help for all of us to come to terms with our feelings for daddy. My very bright and compassionate mom was ahead of her time. Her insights into the needs that we were having could not be met on a professional basis in those days. The Irish had huge and lengthy wakes to let out their feelings: dinners, drinking, and socializing. My mom refused to have an elaborate reception after the funeral with everyone drinking and laughing. In fact she held her feelings inside all of her life. In my estimation, each individual carries bits and pieces of the sad and bad events in our pockets so we continue to learn from them and/or cannot let go.

Norman Berk talked to mom. He found that he was too close to his friend, my daddy, to help like he thought he could. We had all lived in the same house before each family purchased separate homes. The Berks invited us to their farmhouse in the Catskills during the summer months and that became a special event for mom, Kathleen, and me.

Back home, mom and Eileen, Margo's mom, would field phone calls from people who wanted to know how they could be friends when they were of different religions. They were Jewish and we were Catholic. Actually, we had met living in the same apartment-home when mom and Eileen were both pregnant, mom with me and Eileen with Margo. Our friendships have flourished throughout our lives. And so, they educated the callers by saying that they appreciated differences. I was always proud of our acceptance of one to another. I've always enjoyed differences as a result of mom's attitude and the Berk family's presence in my life. Together we explored cultural and intellectual pursuits in addition to the average activities in high school and college. Grandma Ceil, Eileen's mother, was among the first woman to pass the New York City bar exam and become an attorney. Her stands on social justice issues were intriguing and infectious. The children as well as adults all learned from her grand empathy and humanity.

Shortly after dad's death, I came downstairs one morning to eat breakfast. My mother was stirring oatmeal on the kitchen stove. Placing her hand on the countertop in front of the windows that looked out on our beautiful backyard, she turned toward me.

"I caught you touching your personal parts last night. You had your hands down 'there' under the sheets."

I felt queasy and uncomfortable. Those now familiar feelings I didn't know enough to call them anxiety moved up my arms and legs. They were the emotions that happened during family outings when I felt trapped sitting next to my parents in our car. Mom continued in a rigid voice. Uncomfortable, her demeanor switched to resemble a businesswoman.

"I am going to make plans for you to talk to a priest about this problem. I just don't know what to do about it," she admitted.

I knew that she was referring to confession. I would have to be sorry about this problem that I had just discovered myself. I had never heard of masturbation before and could not even pronounce it. Furthermore, remembering the prayers for my father not to return exacerbated some guilt. When I had a lot to confess, the usual behavior was to go over and over my list of sins. It was getting lengthy:

"Bless me father, for I have sinned. I disobeyed my father and talked back to him when I was setting the table in the wrong way; I prayed for my father to go away; I touched myself in a bad place. That's all, father." I hoped to get off with a light penance.

Everything had to be owned up to in the confessional. To make matters worse, mom's plans were to take me to a parish several miles away from our home. There I was to meet with not one but two priests. Apparently, my pleasurable behavior needed to be hidden from our local parish priests and community. A few days later mom informed me that it was time to go for the special confession. My guilt had reached delusional proportions with fears of punishment claiming reality. We arrived at the parish and mom spoke with the first priest alone while I waited. Come to think of it, Kathleen did not have to come along with us. One night, I almost told her about the pleasurable activity. My young intuition told me to forget it. Kathleen was a lucky sister to have a sister like me who kept her out of trouble. I sat in the rectory office terrified.

I was called into the first priest's office. Walking slowly into the room, I sat in front of his desk. As I remember, he was a middle-aged, soft-spoken man. He talked at great length about something. I surely don't remember. My queasy, uncomfortable feelings had turned into a new form of sheer anxiety that made me think my skin would crack from the pressure of internal distress. His final wrap-up was to determine that how I touched myself was a mortal sin. I would have to go to confession to another priest who was waiting in the next room. He would give me absolution and I could avoid going to hell.

An old fashioned confessional screen was set up in the next room just for me. My uncomfortable feelings were on the rise. At least I did not have to go into a confessional box. An elderly priest sat behind the screen. The power of the priests in matters of sex was so very pronounced. We knew nothing. As celibates they were supposed to know nothing, but we honored priestly expertise in an area where vowed to know nothing.

"Bless me Father, for I have sinned," I said sorrowfully. I told him something based on what the last priest said. I don't remember if I confessed praying for my father to go away. I was concentrating on being contrite and honest about the masturbation. With that, the priest looked around the screen. He wanted to know where I touched myself? My mind is blank after his question.

No one remembers exactly what happened in the past. Go to a wedding and compare notes on high school until friends are laughing together. However, I tend to milk very painful memories for all they are worth. I look for what truly happened to reduce the anxieties thus created. I press them down as a masseuse fingers a trigger point until it pops. The above memory lies somewhere between a true memory and one I created, but it was to affect my spirituality for a long time.

Many Saturdays after the arranged, remote confession, I dutifully and unwillingly stood in line at our own church for the required weekly confession. Saturday became purging day. My high states of anxiety made everything look bright. My whole world looked like little tiny pieces of light disintegrating all around me. I knew that I would be relieved if I made a good confession. Forgiveness would bring me closer to Jesus.

"I disobeyed my mother," I began once I was in the confessional. That was easy. Finding more sins got harder. Finally, leaving the box, my small body flooded with relief. Now all I had to do was take a bath. I'd be washed clean, inside and out; Saturday would be over. I was ready for Sunday Mass and could receive Jesus in the Eucharist.

One Saturday mom noticed that I really had trouble with anxiety while I waited in the confession line. She arranged for a parish priest who was good with nervous children to hear my confession. He told me that the angels took sins away from children like me. I was to relax and know that God loved me. If I was not so sure about a sin, I was to give myself the benefit of the doubt. I really liked him. Eventually he died of cancer and I had to go back to the regular priests. Once again, I stood in line overcome with anxiety.

I had become such an odd duck. My friends were home studying or playing. Me? I was chewing my fingernails. I prayed that if I had urinated before coming to church, I had not set any sexual arousal in motion; I would have to consider and reconsider it as possible sin waiting on the confessional line. My list of sins was long enough. I looked so sweet in my grey beret with its red tassel that matched my grey suit. Who would guess I was such an eleven-year old vamp? I looked as if I would barely ever scratch an itch.

I don't remember Kathleen standing in line most Saturdays. Perhaps the anxiety fogged my mind. Margo had it made in the shade. Jewish families didn't go to confession. You had to be Catholic. I was jealous that I was not allowed to go to synagogue and study Hebrew. It was always an understanding between the two families.

They did not go Christmas caroling and I couldn't see the inside of a synagogue. However, we honored each other's traditions. Kathleen and I gave the Berks Hanukkah presents and they gave us Christmas presents. We cherished each other as humans. It ended up providing a great sense of balance for me. I was always looking beyond my anxiety because I knew something else existed.

Earlier in my years, five or six, I played with imaginary friends by the names of Pam and Henry. I could not see them as they existed in my imagination. I would excuse myself from the dinner table in the breezeway and go to a large boulder in front of the yard, off to the side near the neighbor's chain link front gate. Pam and Henry and I pretended that we were statues in an elegant garden. We hoped the cars would understand and notice us. Pam, Henry, and I had lengthy conversations about living on the rock together. Ants lived at the base of the rock. A few times I took a stick (Pam and Henry would never hurt the ants; I had no accomplices) and stuck it in the ants' front door. The ants poured out of their abandon pathways with baby larvae and started to dig a new home.

The adults laughed about my excursions to the boulder with my friends, Pam and Henry. It hurt my feelings. I could feel really sore inside from the hurt. My mother told me years later that they were only enjoying me, but at the time I felt vulnerable and hurt. Sometimes I felt isolated and alone, like a fossil inside of a rock, with the exception of my imaginary friends. I crushed easily. I also felt really guilty about the ant situation. Causing so many live creatures to relocate like I did was grist for my guilt. I never killed one, as killing was a mortal sin. I always stepped over ants even if I'd be late.

"Hurry up, we'll be late," someone would say as I was saving the life of a bug. While I loved all that went on in my yard, Saturday had to roll around. Time, sinfulness, and anxiety became cataclysmic. Only time might bring me back to me.

I don't remember if my brother and sister had to go to the priests after daddy died. Apparently they hadn't committed mortal sins. An occasional flashback to the Empire State Building gave me queasy feelings that I didn't understand. Even my intellectual observations were bruised before he died. A deep and heavy sadness came to live right in the middle of my chest. I was leery of every move I made. Sticking my fingers down my throat for dry, raw undulations and self-hating sensations brought relief from my dilemma of having no place to turn to that felt safe.

My manic-depression, now known as bipolar 1 disorder, was more like a tornado than a hurricane whose path has a broad destruction. A tornado destroys everything in its way when it touches the ground, sometimes with several successful touchdowns but thankfully many areas surrounding it are spared. A tornado is episodic like my childhood bipolarity. There is more hope for rebuilding than after the force and scope of a hurricane. If someone only concentrates on the demolished houses from a tornado or the lives that had to crawl out of the wreckage, then healing will take time. Concentrate on the fields that were spared and the hope of rebuilding, and self-care will move more quickly. I was alive. Initially, that's what it takes to begin self-care in the face of bipolarity, a physical illness.

My family really didn't notice the extremes of the disorder. I began to mask the mood swings by sublimating my depression and anxiety into religious righteousness and concerns. Environmental factors such as daddy's death and the mild brain damage from the sled accident intervened. However, my environment provided me with love and a good home. Bipolar disorder has many physiological components and no cure. To blame the family, without serious psychological reasons, such as physical or sexual abuse, would only add stress. Genetic factors add information to the picture of disease and can alert families to the possibilities for the purpose of finding professional help if necessary.

One evening my mom, Kathleen, and me were reading in the living room of our pretty Cape Cod style home. Those architectural designs were popular in those days in suburbia. They always sported a breezeway. I thought it was the best little home of anyone I knew. We had trees all over the yard, blue iris, ivy, and a blue stone driveway marked by cherry trees. My love of beauty was satisfied and nourished at every turn.

That particular night we heard a noise outside in the bushes. Then the doorbell rang. We opened the door just a crack, but no one was there on the brick doorsteps. The next-door-neighbor's voice flooded us with relief. He had stepped backward into the bushes, and when he saw us he pointed to the sky. There were beautiful, soft lights rising on the horizon. He explained that they were the Aurora Borealis or Northern Lights that could be seen in the northern hemisphere during the summertime. The lights are charged particles emitted from the sun that get caught in the magnetic wells at the magnetic poles caused by the shape of the earth's magnetic field, exciting the air molecules there, and causing them to emit light.

The experience of the Northern Lights facilitated my belief that there were two worlds for me to know: the world of jarring bright lights and these softer ones. One set happened when I also felt like a fossil inside of a rock, and the others were free flowing and unpredictable. Maybe I had those inside of me, too.

CHAPTER 2

Adolescence (1962-1966)

When beach time arrived in 1962, the year after my graduation from eighth grade, I found the perfect bathing suit in a local dress store. I announced that I was going to buy a two-piece bathing suit like all the other eight graders. My mother seemed relieved until we actually arrived on one of the town beaches. I took off my beach cover and revealed a navy blue two-piece suit that only had a sixteenth of an inch between the top and the bottom like shorts. The top piece came up so high that it hit the middle of my neck. It was a few inches above my collarbone. The top resembled the uniforms that the cadets of West Point Academy wear on their parade grounds.

"For heaven's sake, Patricia, you'd reveal more in a one piece bathing suit. Why did you buy it?" mom inquired with frustration.

"Well, it fit the regulations for bathing suits in one of the pamphlets in the back of church," I retorted.

"Oh God!" she said as she looked heavenward and sank back in her beach chair. I knew that she would call her friend, Eileen Berk and moan and complain about my frustrating behavior. Mom and Eileen discussed their daughters all the time.

Meanwhile, I lathered up with suntan lotion and put some on my back. The brochure had not mentioned open backs on girls' bathing suits, so I was safe from sin and repentance. Next I covered my face, arms, and legs. I smiled and waved to my mom and took off down the beach. I planned to get a suntan as I walked along the edge of the salty waves. The lotion protected me from the sting of the salt water and the heat of the sun. For a few fleeting minutes, I was happy. I was living within the guidelines of the Catholic brochures with their rules and regulations. I basked in the sunshine and the safety God's caring provided me that afternoon in my two-piece bathing suit. Happiness was followed by worry for the girls who were exposing their bodies to potential sin in their bikinis. The boys were also in my prayers.

In Catholic school the nuns would talk about sin. I would read all of the pamphlets in the back of church regarding mortal and venial sin. My mother would roll her eyes as she watched me reading pamphlets in the living room. One of the brochures concerned the length of shorts for girls. Bermuda knee length was good for wearing at my age. Mid thigh length was a venial sin and short shorts were a mortal sin. If a boy looked at us in those lengths, he might have impure thoughts, ultimately leading into a state of mortal sin. The girl wearing the short shorts might have a pregnancy out of wedlock. We were not privy to sex education or any understanding that sexual feelings were just feelings. I would go into a tizzy of prickly feelings up and down my arms and legs. Hell fire was my future.

A classmate came to visit me one day. I was still thinking about the shorts pamphlet, so I showed it to her. She didn't say much.

"Let's go ask my mom what she thinks about it," I said to her. Needless to say, on that sweltering hot day, I was wearing Bermuda shorts and a long sleeve shirt that covered me up to my neck.

"Look mom, it says in these brochures that we can not wear certain shorts," as I showed her the brochure. I explained the dynamics of sinful short wearing. My friend was beginning to giggle. Mom looked vexed with lines appearing across her forehead.

"Oh, Patricia! This looks a little severe, sweetheart! You can certainly wear mid-length in the heat," she replied with despair in her voice.

"No," I replied emphatically.

Patricia Frisch, Ph.D.

"Look at the rules on page two," I continued. My friend came around less and less frequently after my rigorously precise short shorts rendition.

"You are so weird," she said when I saw her at school one day. I felt sad and alone with my rigid moral vision. My growth and development continued on its lopsided pathway. The pre-teen and teen years with its age appropriate tasks were sent scurrying into dark corners because I lacked adaptive abilities.

Anxious and depressed feelings interfered with reality like a knitter dropping stitches originally intended for making a perfect garment. The normal knit two and pearl one learned in a family circle of women didn't match my knitter's patterning. Mood swings distorted the fine piece of cloth, swelling my hands as they attempted to make a beautiful garment.

Some reality coupled with coagulated emotions made me feel dizzy as I attempted to remain in the circle of women knitters. Mood swings grabbed life's knitted patterns. They tossed reality up and down but not too far away from looking like a normal garment. The other women in the knitting circle encouraged me to pick up the dropped stitches and try again. No one guessed how much it was taking me to knit as I approximated sweater making closely. I shook with tension while thinking that my knitting equaled that of a sinful person. Mood swings were becoming the garments that I would wear.

My adolescent years were punctuated and permeated by my religious preoccupations and entangling my growth process. I was guilt ridden about the prayers I had said the night before my daddy's death. I wanted God to take him away from me because he was always correcting me. Memories of priests scared me. Tensely, I strove for a perfection that would free me from sin, disturbing thoughts, and increase my chances of bringing my daddy back to life. Constant anxiety filled my mind, twisted my vision, and reinforced that I was a sinful nobody.

Daddy's death was only the beginning of my problems with guilt. It was couched in anxiety and was more than I could handle, compromising my thought process. As the guilt continued to claim me, I asked God for a favor: please give me a sign that I had not been responsible for his death. I had knelt down and prayed to God that my father would not come home and discipline me anymore. It was like the jump from the Empire State Building that I had forgotten about. I wished to escape feelings inside of me, not so much the person. The environmental affect seemed stronger for me than most people. If the Sunday newspaper had an accident on the front cover, then I was guilty. If not, then I was free. I got up that next Sunday morning and nervously took a peek.

"NO!" I softly screamed to myself. A car accident was the biggest news story on the front page of the Sunday news, the Lord's Day. The guilt and anxiety climbed higher, making my skin feel prickly. I still had some cognitive reality left. I mused to myself.

"This is a bad indication. I should not have done this to myself." At the same time, my inside walls of sanity were dropping. I never considered talking to my mom, Eileen Berk, Margo, or a nun at school. The original desire to jump off the Empire State Building never caused me to seek an adult's help either. I kept it inside, probably overwhelmed by the anxiety and its symptoms.

I started to hate the sound of newspaper as people relaxed and enjoyed reading them. They would crack the paper, making crisp sounds as they turned the pages. I could not relax around my family, just like I could not end my tension in the car on family trips. I had to leave the living room. Calculating every step I took, I developed an overbearing awareness of my body. It overwhelmed my rational thinking. I could not relax anywhere; neither in the living room on Sunday mornings, not watching my mother take a nap on the living room sofa. My belief that I was bad enough to go to hell for my father's death, plus the fear of confession, caused generalized anxiety. I felt queasy even when people were relaxing, smiling, or enjoying each other's company.

By contrast, I enjoyed certain areas of life, such as dance and sailing. I would strive diligently to reach a goal. I cherished striving to accomplish something when the anxiety was gone. I continued to strive to reach goals in school and other activities.

I apparently came across to adults as getting by in life but odd. The sadness of losing my daddy appeared as a normal reaction. No one approached me about the connections destroying my peace of mind. I continued to find ways to hide inside myself.

Self-rejection, due to the terrible things I had done, brought an overly sensitive reaction to what people said to or about me. I was driven for ambivalent reasons to do good deeds. My idealism developed from many wonderful spiritual thoughts but also the hope of bring daddy back. I would be free from the damning thoughts of hell.

At the eighth grade graduation ceremony, we all sang the words to Panis Angeligus and to a few other inspirational lyrics I barely remember. The more we practiced, the more I could envision my mission in life. With my mood swings, I vowed over and over to never sin against Jesus for even the slightest offense.

My fingers moved all the time as I counted my sins entwined with the rosary beads. I needed to know the exact number of sins when I went to confession. The time between confessions after graduation seemed less and less important. Staying in the state of grace was the crux of the matter. I found a nice size picture of Jesus, morbid, depressing, and crucified to hang over my bed.

On the positive and spiritual side of life, having good relationships did happen at times. For example, Harold was a tall, refined, and good-looking boy that everyone liked in the eighth grade class. One day the other kids told me that Harold was writing my name all over his notebook. He was going to ask me out. I guessed that his present girlfriend would not like it one bit. Normally, I would have felt an allegiance to her when he asked me out.

However, it was common knowledge that in the fall he was going into the seminary to become a priest.

He was very devout. He was even going to take the vow of silence to devote his life to God alone. The adults all admired Harold very much because he knew what he wanted to do. The rest of us hadn't grown up yet like Harold. With a little hint of sarcasm, they'd tell the rest of us that we could learn from his maturity. No girl had dibs on him. I was ready with my answer when he asked me out.

He called one afternoon on our phone in the hallway across from the Fibber McGee closet. His voice sounded rich and deep. He said he'd like to take me out.

"Yes, I'd love to go," I said. I also thought how wonderful it was that someone so interested in religion would ask me out on a date.

Harold's mother drove him to my house one summer's morning. We were going to sun ourselves on their family boat with another couple from our graduating class. We headed down my street to the harbor at the bottom of the hill from where I lived. His mother had packed a picnic lunch to take on the boat. We got into a dinghy and rowed out to the motorboat anchored in the harbor. The four of us had a fantastic day of laughing and splashing around in the water.

In the late afternoon, Harold motioned for me to climb up on top of the main section of the boat to sit with him. We sat together until he slid across the boat top and turned away from me. I sat very still because I didn't know what he wanted. He was silent. He kept looking up at the sky and finally he reached back and held my hand. I realized that he was praying. The prayers involved me. I wondered if he was speaking with God about the life he would never have. He would be giving up the possibility of a wife and children.

"I want to go down now with our friends in the boat," he said.

"Okay," I said. I slid down the slippery side of the boat, squeaking all of the way.

Patricia Frisch, Ph.D.

During the summer months leading up to his departure for the order of priests he had chosen, he would ask me out to one of the many graduation parties. Never again did he seem so serene or mature as that moment on top of the boat. He seemed boyish while talking and laughing with the other boys at the parties. Sometimes we hardly spoke to each other; we were just together. I, of all the girls, understood that nobody owned him.

He belonged to Jesus. In September, he was gone. He was the first goodbye I'd said since I was ten and daddy died. I moved along to the ninth grade in public school. So much was happening in school that I must admit forgetting about him for years on end. I was capable of letting go. I had an ability that would be to my advantage someday.

Slowly but surely, I was burying my early symptoms of anxiety. I learned ways to relate to the other students in a very shy and guarded way. I had a few friends and I was getting by. I knew I was not keeping in step with everyone academically or socially, but I wasn't a disaster case. I was placed in average classes because the Catholic elementary school education was considered inferior to the public elementary school programs. If we were allowed into the top classes, it was because we earned them in the average classes. I could participate in the classroom atmosphere but barely in the halls and lunch areas. I was always a sensitive outsider looking in on conversations.

At the same time, I was also manufacturing some weak and almost useless ways of perceiving life. Painful feelings of rejection mounted as I moved about the junior high and senior high campuses. I did not understand how come boys did not ask me out on dates or dance with me at parties. It might have been my unapproachable looks and grimaces (or the Bermuda shorts). I thought myself responsible for this fact and everything that went wrong. Mea culpa, it was my fault everyday of school.

If a boy spoke to me, I couldn't say hi. I remember the emerald green satin dress I wore to the ninth grade dance. It was a hand-me-down from our cousins. I didn't really like it and felt out of place. Nobody asked me to dance anyway. Gone was the security of summer graduation parties with a safe group of friends. My mother really pushed me to ask a boy to the Sadie Hawkins Dance my sophomore year. I cringed for weeks at the thought of asking a boy in reverse of the usual dances.

I asked someone. I didn't think he was good looking, so it was easier to approach him. He accepted, and four of us went together to the high school gym. Slow dancing was more than I had bargained for. We had Marrying Sam marry us, and I had a small yellow ring on my finger. Scared enough, I had asked mom about kissing and hugging. She was vague about the details. My date told my friend that he really liked me but he never asked me out. He went to church like I did; however, he was also advanced for a good Catholic girl like me. I decided I didn't need confession for this date.

Our closest family of friends, the Berks, usually saved the bottom from falling out of my adolescence. I was taken seriously. The parents understood more about humanity than I did with my severe scrupulosity. Because I was a Catholic, I had to continue struggling with my salvation while they attended to the present moment. The Berks gave me a window to another approach in life. The parents got along well with my mom and they were a great support to her, like a family would do for someone in widow's shoes.

Another saving grace in adolescence was my dancing. With an invitation to teach dance at the age of ten, I excelled at what I was teaching. The environment thrilled me. I went into New York City for dance conventions where I took lessons from a ballet master who tapped my ankles when they were in the wrong position. We danced in ballrooms that were exhilarating. It was hot dancing in a leotard and tights so I forgot about the low cut leotard. My toe shoes ran away from the pain of growing up. Parental approval all added up to the happiest package of my adolescence.

In time, I had to decide if trying out for a major ballet company might lead to a career choice. My teacher, a well-known choreographer, wanted me to try. The frustration of barre work, where we exercised our legs and arms by holding onto a barre fastened along the wall, contributed largely to my decision to say no, turn aside, and go to college. The frustration was greater than the pleasure or the goals that most dancers find rewarding. Standing at the barre with no music for a half an hour had no diversion. The tiny batting exercises done at the feet were precise and very focused. I wanted to cry or scream for the ballet mistress to at least break the monotony with some music. She never would because we were developing focused physical self-discipline. It would hold us in good stead when we danced on the floor. Also, it assured that our legs and feet were warmed up against the possibility of accidents.

My intolerance of pain was perhaps because of the manic side of manic-depressive. Manic can make my joints and muscles feel like they are turning to steel. I blamed lack of self-discipline for resultant irritability and frustration. Self-hatred sadly filled in the lack of knowledge base for what was transpiring. Long faces replaced the drama of Debussy and Chopin at the barre. Another note in the decision-making process came when I was studying jazz in New York City. My mom suggested I try out for some Broadway shows or traveling shows.

"It will give you an idea of the competition and the job market," she said. I found a call for a traveling version of *Brigadoon*. We went to the audition together. Right away, I realized that I was the wrong shape. Brigadoon needed busty women dancers. I was petite. I took one turn across the floor.

"Thank you," said the choreographer. Mom was an extrovert, and she put her orientation to good use in the waiting room. She had lots to tell me on the car ride home.

Most of the dancers were starving. $80 was the top weekly salary. Someone else was giving up their apartment due to lack of funds.

When I was eighteen, I wanted a sailboat in the worst way. What could have lead to a major depression was averted by sailing and its saving graces. I saw a sailfish, the smallest of sailboats, advertised in the local newspaper. The neighbor across the street who had sailing experience accompanied me to the advertised address. The sailboat was made of marine plywood, and painted a beautiful shade of blue with white sails to complete her beauty.

Polarized

When my neighbor spoke to the boat owner, he was overly persuasive. Explaining that my dad had died and there wasn't much money to go around, could the owner cut the cost in half? Besides, marine plywood was heavy and not a good sail. He would have to help me learn to sail it. The gentleman gave in to the soap opera presentation, and we loaded the sailboat onto his truck. We headed home with a little sailboat of questionable quality and/or ability.

My neighbor never did help me to sail; I taught myself. I loved puttering around in the bay, crossing it, and staying out until sunset. What my little boat lacked in construction was filled with imagination. It provided the wind for my sails as well as speed and power. Forward-looking beliefs about life helped my mind soar with the seagulls. My spirit moved much swifter than the heavy plywood sailfish.   Friends sailed her, scrape her barnacles, and rose above the usual complaints sailors might have about the condition of her sails or her very slow turnabout.

My emotions knew the exhilaration of breezes in her sails and the joy of sitting on top of deep and still waters. It was like being in my soul. She stirred my spirit of adventure and gave me the peaceful space to dream my dreams and imagine practical goals. Sailing along the waters of life, I was free.

I started to keep a journal that I left in the drawer of my desk for Kathleen to find. I placed a note on it for her before I went to college. When I returned, she had written a note back to me. She stated that she was glad to read it because she never knew what was going on with me. I had freely given it to her to find (in my desk drawer) and guilt never allowed me to assert myself with a request for reciprocal information. I was generous to a fault. I was Christian, but generosity was easier than asking for what I needed or wanted.

All in all, mom was a good mother who wanted the best for her daughters. Like many parents, a single parent at that, she strained and had troubles accepting that she could not provide everything for us in this life. She couldn't make us happy. We had to find what we needed and wanted in life by ourselves. Preparing children to help themselves is a tedious and complex task.

"Nobody prepares you for raising children. All I have is what my mother did," she would say quite often. We do have many more educational opportunities for parents today, and I believe that my mother wanted a full life for her children. She prayed often and did her best. I have few negative feelings about her efforts.

Mom took us faithfully to our little old stone church. It meant a lot to me when it came to the sacraments and devotion. My earliest recollection is of Kathleen's baptism. My daddy's funeral was held there. I received my first Communion in a white dress and veil in that old stone church. I wore a red gown the day I received Confirmation by the bishop. The Knights of Columbus walked down the aisle crossing their swords, making a passageway for the bishop. Only one fly in the ointment was my first confession.

Kathleen tried out for the choir and was the only one that the nuns rejected. I felt badly for her although I gathered she didn't care. I was accepted and the choir director decided I was to sing alto. Everything we sang was in Latin, as the changes in the Catholic liturgies of Vatican II had not gone into effect. I had to climb up the old rickety staircase to the choir loft. The walls smelled of almost one hundred years of incense burning. We would climb down the ancient winding stairs to go to Communion and everyone knew we were the choir members.

I hated it when the priests announced that the old church was to be torn down. The staircase was roped off because it was dangerous. I found the whole process to be very sad. It was a place I associated with my daddy. Tearing it down sent him further away from me. A new church was built across the street. It was grand and beautiful. Latin Mass passed away for Mass in English. The priest stood out side of church to shake everyone's hands. I belonged to the youth group that decided what social ministries we were to be involved in for the church.

I organized and led a discussion one night between the black and white people of our town. It was the 1960's and race relations were front-page news. The south saw black people sitting in drugstores wanting to be served, demonstrating, and riding in the front of buses. Many white people walked with them as black people spoke up for their rights. We had a multicultural confrontation for openers. Two hundred people showed up from both sides of town to air their differences. The woman who was supposed to speak came to the coffee shop were I was working and begged off.

"You could do a better job and I have a sore throat," she said with a shaky voice. So now I was scared about another part I had to play that night, but I did it.

The list of problems included the fact that all of the stores on the black side of town had been torn down for urban renewal that never happened. People who lived in the neighborhoods behind the torn down area were stranded. They had lived there all of their lives and now they had to spend money on bus fare to get to the stores. There were no recreational facilities on the black side of town. An angry white man with a red face stood up and pointed his finger at the black leader from the youth center.

"Your people should not play on our ball fields and playgrounds. You should build your own," he yelled. The sparks flew for two hours. A panel was formed consisting of town officials to further discuss the differences.

The priest in charge of our church ministry group thought I could do anything after that evening. That felt good but I also had inklings of how much work he might expect. Anyone interested from the church ministry group attended lectures in other churches with similar formats. An enormous amount of energy was going into the effort to right the social injustice being done to the black people in our community.

I still felt as if I was waiting for the world to begin. I survived the depressing times by escaping them. I didn't want to be near mom or other people at all. My imagination became a great aide in running away. I could daydream all sorts of pleasant and sometimes morbid things to entertain myself. With racing thoughts, I could always sail away in a kind of motion that always made me feel better.

CHAPTER THREE

College (1966-1970)

It was a special moment when Uncle James came to help mom with her finances on a humid August afternoon in 1966. He was very knowledgeable about bank accounts, the NY stock market, and how to work with a widow's finances. We were fortunate to have an uncle who had a business head on his shoulders. I just knew that his visits with mom were a significant factor toward continuing to live in our beautiful environment.

Tea with ice tinkling inside green colored glasses barely soothed the heat in our backyard as mom and Uncle James droned on and on about the business at hand. I sat quietly wearing my graduation dress of white pique embossed with white flowers. I enjoyed thinking about my dress, as I fashioned it myself. Aunt Jan had taught me to make my own clothes.

"Anna, get your daughter a sewing machine because she has talent," said my aunt.

So one Christmas morning I discovered a blue and white sewing machine under the tree. It was up to me to maintain this wonderful machine. It sported a variety of needles and a silver plate on the machine top. I could open the plate and oil the gears. I dusted it often and put the blue and white top on each night. I didn't mind the discipline at all. It was a challenge I could handle, and it afforded me time to be alone. My solitude taught me about my ability to sew and like myself. It was a challenge I could handle.

Polarized

A trip to the fabric store was a jaunt that I looked forward to once in awhile when I had saved my babysitting money. Once home, scissors cut fashionable patterns. I loved whizzing the bright colors over the silver plate for the needle to stitch together. For most of the time I spend at the sewing machine, I had a good self-concept. I commanded my bright and colorful world. Only when I was fatigued would stray thoughts create frustration and self-hatred. Only once did I pull the garment away from the needle and throw it across the room. Sewing didn't block my problems. It showed me that I could pull the threads of my life and create anew. The Northern Lights were in my mind as I finally stitched my little life together.

The afternoon my uncle visited I was drinking in excitement about leaving for college. I smoothed my white dress over and over feeling the embossed flowers. It kept me from jumping up and leaving the very important meeting that I was politely observing from time to time. While seated in my chair on the back lawn with mom and Uncle James, I drifted away, lost in all that had taken place in the past year.

I felt mortified for four years at the secular local high school that I deemed useless and valueless; a Catholic university caused my veins to fill with soaring joy. I was ready for the release. Just to make sure that my decision about college was from God; I spoke to the eighth grade nun I admired, Sister Mary, about entering the convent. She wisely offered alternatives. I might fit in another part of the church as the laity was becoming more active. I needed to go to college first anyway to enter the order.

It was an ordeal during the past year to apply and finally be accepted to college. The admissions counselor caused a mix-up. She only sent some applications for each student, and thus I received rejection letters from two colleges. She had not sent in my application to the school that I really wanted. Mom was angry and frustrated. As a single mother who was denying herself many extras and saving her money to send three of us to college, she wondered what had happened. Mom was not good at confronting authority, preferring deference, and believing that everyone tried their best.

My applications were a counselor-mess-up for sure, but it was late to do anything except send in the right application and hope for the best.

My grades were in the B range, nothing special. I despaired because I thought that I was not a preferred student in the guidance office. I continued to label myself as nobody special, feeling hurt and depressed. It coincided with mom's assessment that God had sent her three average children with no unusual problems for her to deal with. I wondered where her perception came from and if the mild depression that I lived with everyday would follow me into new endeavors.

While waiting to hear anything from school, I went down to the beach and walked barefoot with occasional glances skyward. My eyes winced in the sun. If I didn't get into the school I wanted, it was too late to apply anywhere else.

"I guess, God, that you want me to be an average person going nowhere," was all the faithfulness I could muster. With frustration in my legs and arms, I crunched the oyster shells scattered over the beach and eventually returned to mom's old, blue Ford Falcon. I turned on the key and took my time going home. Aimlessly I tried taking in as much green scenery as I could. I turned the blue Falcon into our blue stone driveway and pulled to a stop. I sat staring into space through the ivy covering the chain link fence alone the driveway. Mom looked serious as she opened the front door. A letter had come from the college I wanted to attend. I hurriedly opened it up, and it was an acceptance. I wrinkled it to my chest as I truly thanked God that I might have a chance to count in this world. My family really celebrated that night with a special dinner. Education was special to daddy and his family.

For once in my life my chances for adventure were starting to increase abundantly. The afternoon on the beach was agony; I was mesmerized by nature on the way home; and then I had feelings of ecstasy. I was in an extraordinary state of mind, tinged with the guilt that I didn't deserve such happiness. If the happiness grew too strong as the night progressed, I might commit a sin and have to confess. I loathed those extra feelings that always dragged me down at a high moment. I had to examine my conscience to decide if too much happiness was a sign of sin. However, I felt secure that night that I would be safe at a Catholic university.

That afternoon, sitting outside with mom and Uncle James, my brother walked swiftly through the breezeway door. He abruptly stated that he was ready to take me to school the next morning. An Irishman of few words like my father, he ushered in my moment of leave-taking. I had a dramatic rush of excitement and tears for finally leaving home. I was about to say goodbye to my home where I grew up and everything was familiar. My new college adventure at the university of my choice was just a day away.

That last evening held a passage I didn't want to make. Mom asked me to have a cup of tea and sit on the sofa in the living room. She looked especially energetic in a green knit outfit shimmering next to her red hair. As soon as I sat myself down on the sofa cushions, tears welled up in my eyes. She wanted to say good-bye, recounting all of our days together. She was the one who held me when I cried about daddy being gone. Tension welled up inside as I was now the next in line to leave her. A few months before my daddy died, her mother who had lived with us died. My brother was away most of the time and now I had to go. She and Kathleen were left behind to become a new family. College was my lifeline to new ways of being. I would leave behind some ambivalent feelings, but now I wanted mom to know she had done a good job as a mother. Guilt collided with love. With a rash of anxiety, I gulped down my tea as if I could rush the conversation to a pleasant ending.

"You're coming back, right?" Mom asked.

"Of course, Mom, Thanksgiving is not too far away," I said compassionately.

"Well," She continued.

" I – I'll keep your sewing machine in the corner of the dining room for you. I'll buy some material and a pattern if you wish," she said with hope in her voice.

"Mom, you and I can go shopping when I land at La Guardia Airport. We can go to the material store on the way home," her face looking like a well of love almost swallowed by sadness. We hugged. She said what she always said to her children.

"I love yah," with her mixture of sadness and love. It was a melancholy way of trying to let go.

Separation would lead to new connections. I comforted myself that my brother was driving me to the university that was also his alma mater. He left home for college eight years ago when daddy died, making trips home at holidays. Working during the summers, my older sibling lived with my uncles, aunts, and cousins. Necessity, time, and distance meant we were not really part of the same family. It was kind of him to take this trip and save mom the effort. In a few years, Kathleen followed me to the same university.

I helped my brother pile my belongings into his car, and I waved good-byes to mom and Kathleen. I was crying as we pulled out of the blue stone driveway leaving the house and the beautifully treed yard of my youth. My brother rode in silence all the way through the familiar side streets of my town, and out on to the open highway leading us to the university.

"Can I go to the bathroom?" as I couldn't wait any longer to ask.

"Can't you hold it another hour?" he asked.

"No, can't we stop?" I pleaded.

Reluctantly, he agreed. About forty-five minutes later he pulled into a gas station. Shortly after that stop he pulled off the side of the road and said that he was going to take a nap. He pulled a Scottish red plaid blanket out of the trunk and laid it down in the grass. Silence ensued. I walked around and sat on the fender. In about half an hour, he pulled up the blanket and crawled behind the steering wheel.

As we drew near to the destination, I started to cry.

"What's the matter?" he inquired.

"I'm scared," I replied.

"Oh come now," he answered with a mixture of love and irritation.

"This is supposed to be fun," he smiled.

We drove into a suburban community of small houses and pulled into someone's driveway. He turned to me.

"We are having dinner with my friends, old college classmates," he said. I told myself to make the best of it because this is fun.

Suddenly, his demeanor changed. He was friendly, laughed, and talked with his friends. One side of my brother was the silent Irishman so typical of our family. The other one was a charming extrovert. His friends were just as glad to see him. They were friendly extroverts. The three of them were catching up on old times and were cordial to me as his little sister. They asked questions about my studies at the university where they had fond memories. Soon dinner was over. He was going to stay with them, but I didn't know that yet. He told me to get back in the car, and he drove me to the dormitory. It was early and I didn't think that many coeds would be registering. I didn't want to bring dishonor to this trip my brother had agreed to take on. I was proud of it, but I had to ask.

"Why can't I stay with you?" I mustered all the self-confidence I had.

" I am going back to my friends' house and you are going to the dorm," he replied. I pleaded my case one more time that I didn't care to stay alone in the dorm.

"You'll be safe," he assured me as he gave me a kiss good-bye. Without answering me, he was gone.

Mom always taught me that Irish men had deep feelings that they didn't always show to the rest of us. When she was engaged to daddy, he and my uncles always visited their parents faithfully. They would kiss their mother in the kitchen and then sit down with their dad and crack open the newspaper. With little conversation, they went every Sunday to the brownstone house in which they were raised. On the way to school, I understood her lessons.

That evening, I managed to meet a few women on my dorm floor. I had already donned my floor length pink bathrobe with a pattern of red flowers. No one ever knows much about new people. I saw myself as about the same speed, wholesome, and not traveling in the fast lane. My sweet, naïve bath-wrap was noticed that night and often giggled about in the following months at casual gatherings in third floor dorm rooms. That night I eventually went to my room and unpacked my suitcases. I felt better after meeting a few friends but remained a little nervous. I took my pink plastic box for toiletry articles and headed for the bathroom. I thought about mom and all the school stuff we had shopped for together. I felt a little homesick. I wanted to call her, but to save money, my brother said he would place a phone call to home from his friend's house before he left. Right then money didn't matter. I fearfully obeyed his wish anyway.

My roommate had not come that night. I turned out the florescent overhead lights and crawled into my freshly made bed. I could see a hazy full moon outside my window. Relaxed and amazed about my new adventure, I decided that my brother was at least right about being safe and comfortable. The next day my roommate with long red hair popped her head in the door.

"Are you Patricia?" she asked while smiling.

"Yes," I said. Being very tall, she bounced around the room in long strides.

"My name is Frankie." I liked her positive energy right away, but didn't know yet about her weakness for cigarettes. As she brought in her suitcases, I noticed that she had lit up. I hated confrontations, especially in my personal space. My stomach was queasy, and I felt such weakness at not knowing if it was okay to openly distain her habit.

"Oh, you smoke," I was able to muster.

Getting along was important to me, too. We each had a side of the room to live in. Her side included cigarettes. Breathing in foul cigarette air was the norm for trying to sleep at night. I talked to our floor advisor who told me to ask her nicely to smoke outside of our room. However, it was not against dorm regulations to smoke in the rooms. I loved so many things about going to college that I decided to put up with the smoking issue that came with a really bright roommate. After a couple of months coeds were drifting into our room and lighting up, playing music. The frustration catapulted me to complain to them, but they convinced me that I needed to learn how to smoke. By the end of the first year, it was my bad habit, too. Our room was always going to be filled with my roommate's foul cigarette air. This way, it was my own smoke.

Besides adjusting to roommates, the first week of school was for orientation and get together parties on campus. The first night I met a pleasant, round-shaped Italian boy, Paul. He asked me out for seven nights in a row. Seven dates were more than I had had in my whole life. To say I was a tad thrown off guard is the truth. Giggling became my defense mechanism. I became manic by the third date. I was probably going to marry him. The girls on the third floor were very amused. Some of them harkened back to our first meeting, innocent in my pink bathrobe with red roses. I turned my back on their fun because I was too fascinated with Paul.

However, on the fourth date, my hurt from high school years of not dating and the fear of encountering Paul sexually slowed me down. He looked more like a human being than an angel. This perception continued until the last evening at the mush rush in front of the dorm.

The mush rush was a notorious event at the women's dorm. When it was curfew for the women's dormitory, all the couples who were on dates, plus the student's who were coming in from the bars (where a light 3.2 beer was served to college students) and off campus parties, converged on the front lawn of the dorm for a last good-bye to their date. From a distance it looked like a block party. It was really fun. It was named mush because couples were hugging and kissing goodnight, and rush for running inside before the nuns rang the bell for curfew. The nuns would leave us alone unless there was drunken or immoral sexual behavior going on in the crowd.

On the last date, Paul pulled me close during the mush rush and tried to stick his tongue in my mouth. Alarmed, wanting to appear aloof when I was really shy and puzzled, I shoved his magnificent appendage, the male tongue, back inside his mouth.

"Thanks for a great week," I said and ran inside before sister rang the bell. I took the elevator up to the third floor and ran to find Frankie. I told her what happened.

"French kissing, or tongue kissing, is an invitation to a lower invasion, also a mortal sin," she said with nun like authority. Alas, I had put a dent in my naiveté. Drawing away and going deep inside myself, I was embarrassed. Breathing in the smoky air of our room, Frankie had covered the whole situation. Half asleep, I reminded myself that I did not deserve a week of dates with Paul. I was an almost sinner when his tongue licked my lips. Sin on a Catholic campus had just shown its ugly roots. The next morning I ran to the other end of the third floor looking for a coed from my dates' hometown. I found her.

" You know your friend, Paul, that I've been dating?" She replied.

"Yes." I said.

"Tell him to keep his tongue inside his mouth because tongue-kissing is a mortal sin." I managed to say it with some of my courage and Frankie's. Paul's friend barely flexed a muscle.

"Oh, sure," she said starring at me. I walked away and we never struck up an acquaintance after that incident. I felt odd because I hardly knew what to say or do when it came to sex. I was rigorously and rigidly exact. My mission was to do what was right to avoid hell.

I was more naive than most and willing to listen to other women in the dorm who told me right from wrong in the sexual area. It was not public knowledge if couples were sleeping together; there was no general knowledge of pregnancies or abortions.

In the 1960's on a college campus the average coed's experience included a healthy interest in the opposite sex, but the authorities on campus discouraged any heavy engagement in sexual activity. It was at least hidden by the college students. Lots of drinking dotted weekend events. Drugs only arrived on the scene in my senior year and then mostly marijuana. Homosexuality was not seen overtly and barely discussed. From a liberal standpoint, our era was sensitive to race relations due to the civil rights era, working for equality for black people. The words we hear today such as multiculturalism and homosexual rights were not yet coined. Demonstrations could center on doing away with 3.2 beers because men could go to war at eighteen but not drink real beer until twenty-one. Today's college campus is a far cry from the 1960's. The seeds of today's thinking started with us. I went to Woodstock in search of peace, not drugs, along with many other students hoping to bring justice to all humans: a guttural, groping beginning like Helen Keller pronouncing the word "water."

By the last evening of our seven dates, neither Paul nor I were in love anymore. We parted ways, although we often smiled and waved at each other as we trucked across campus to our classes.

I continued to have a lot of dates while other women on the third floor got to know each other in the dorm. For the autumn dance, I had two boys call and ask me to be their date. I tried not to announce my good fortune during the dorm gatherings in someone's room. I was silent even though I was a little manic. One night I took a phone call for a dance invitation. When I returned to the gathering someone ask me what it was. When I told them, someone said:

"You already have a date to that dance." We all smiled quietly. Their frustrated voices were spiced with some malice at my betrayal. It was enough to make me feel guilty. I also never understood what had made the difference between no dates in high school and an abundance of dates in college. Granted, I smiled and laughed a lot more; I had space to be myself away from the melancholy atmosphere at home since daddy's death.

During freshman orientation week, we were encouraged to sign up for college services by checking boxes on a questionnaire. I checked the one for counseling. I had never gone to a psychological counseling session in my whole life. I was curious, but I didn't think I had anything to be upset about at this time of great learning.

I secured an appointment and really liked Dr. Ann, a woman in her thirties, blond hair, hazel eyes, and a handsome face. She was well groomed, a tad cold and distant, yet soft-spoken. She listened, wanting to know how everything was going in my classes, dorm, and social life. We had a nice conversation, and she invited me to come back whenever I needed to just talk about how things were unfolding at college. I called my mom and told her about the kind psychotherapist. My mom said that she was happy to hear I had someone nice to talk to when I felt the need.

Focusing on each area of my new life, I continued to do well on all of Dr. Ann's fronts. The first real conflict came in the dormitory. Peer pressure started to crack my thin but happy veneer. It all started with wanting the window ajar to get fresh air because of my roommate's smoke. It led to my desire to balance the control.

I made an appointment with Dr. Ann. She talked to me about the differences between individual and peer development. We talked about what I wanted to accomplish and how to value those things compared to giving into group pressure. She eventually told me that she was a developmental psychologist. I still check out growth and development issues in my life today. I find it quite beneficial in focusing myself and understanding other's deficiencies and strengths. I continued to request fair breathing habits in my room despite peer pressure.

As freshman year wore on, I was doing well in all of Dr. Ann's categories and checklists. Nonetheless, I would become very depressed and not know why. I would go back to see her and she would say:

"I don't know where the depressed and anxious feelings are germinating." She could not attach my depressed moods to any particular events because I was doing so well. She prescribed an anti-anxiety medication. I took the meds and went to the cafeteria for some dinner. All of a sudden, I started to think that everything was funny. People enjoyed my special laugh, so nobody at my table seemed to mind. When it was my turn to get in the food line, I grabbed a tray and as I moved up the line, I started slamming it down on the tray's roller bars. I was having so much fun. I did it over and over again, laughing loudly. Frankie grabbed my tray. She knew about my medication and said:

"I think you have had too much of your medicine. Why not go upstairs and lie down for awhile?" I did what she said only because I really thought she was smart. Perhaps I was starting to depend on her too much. In any event, just for that moment, I listened to her. The next day, I went back to see Dr. Ann.

"Well," she sighed, "Those pills were not the answer." She made no reference to the time needed to take effect. She was baffled. I don't know who was supposed to figure out my moods except me. I looked back over my life. If my childhood mission was to bring my father back from the dead, I could do anything by myself. I didn't need the help of a doctor who was awfully nice but not too insightful.

My refusal to let go of negative patterns snagged me, too. I did not consider another therapist because I had other expenses, and Dr. Ann's services were free. I relied on my friends in the dorm to guide me as they had some of the same problems. I'd also smoke and cry every time I broke up with a boy, which was quite often. Then I'd be asked out again and again. It was mood swinging brought to me by the opposite sex. Daddy would flash through my mind sometimes. Mom used to say that someday I'd probably marry someone like my daddy. This thought of a potential marriage relationship that might end in my husband dying early and leaving me to raise children alone brought on more anxiety and closed a door inside of me. In a daze, I visualized memories of my daddy raking leaves in the autumn sun that he and mom would burn at the edge of the road.

Nonetheless, I remember feeling the most intense insecurity around my female friends. Like hating my reflection in a mirror when I was little, the same sex touched my weaknesses more deeply and fully. I tried not to have these anxieties because they were disturbing. I covered them up like leaves swirling and sliding to touch the ground. My popularity with the boys became my denial of any problems with other women.

I tried new adventures despite the growing anxieties. I ran for sophomore class representative to the student body. The winner had 600 votes and I was in last place with 295. I hated politics by the time it was over, yet I was thrilled that 295 people believed in me to do such a responsible job. I didn't know that many people. It was a thrill I never wanted to repeat.

I amassed dates with boys, as many as five in the same weekend. Boys would usually spend their money on the first date or two, and then a library date followed. Hugging in the library stacks became acceptable to my rigid principles. Kisses among the books were safe. The Sunday dates were the most helpful to my budget. A Sunday morning date meant going to Catholic Mass and then breakfast at the local diner. A second date with someone else would include Sunday Mass in the evening plus supper at the same hamburger diner. The combination dates saved me from purchasing a weekend meal ticket. I would save mom money that she usually sent.

I was responsible about my studies and they came easily to me. I was happy about the pleasant and supportive atmosphere. I would concentrate on the many boys that liked and respected me if I was feeling poorly about my self-concept. Academics starved off those anxieties Dr. Ann could not connect with anything.

By process of elimination, I began to discover what disciplines held my attention. Thus, sophomore year I applied for and was accepted into an advanced elementary school teaching tract for good students. It was experimental and would last all junior year. Although it would take me away from the campus that I loved, I felt singled out when I was accepted. I was making strides in life. Academics and dating kept me going forward.

During my second semester of sophomore year, Brad, a very handsome, cool young man asked me out. I was shocked because he was too smooth and sophisticated for me. He could have gone out with a homecoming queen. I was nervous when he picked me up. It was an okay evening. We went to the movies and out for a drink. He was mild mannered and didn't push his affection on me all evening.

At the same time a friend of mine, Tim, asked me out. From a party to the favorite pizza parlor, his obvious gay orientation matched what friends had already told me. We came back to the dorm and climbed up on the roof of the ROTC building across from the dormitory. The mush rush had already begun. Friends were pointing at us and laughing as if we were very different because we were not hugging and kissing. I had no sexual feelings toward him yet he and I were happily philosophizing about life. We never did pay any attention to our friends' laughter. I was the center of his brilliance and loved it.

Brad asked me if he could come over on a Sunday afternoon to just sit around. We landed in the lobby of the dorm. He was very quiet. After awhile he said,

"Look, there is a pot in the boys dormitory for whoever can get you in bed first. You understand?" he said, as he looked at me sideways. He continued, "Whoever beds you down first gets all of the money." He looked at me full face and said,

"I give up."

I sat there stunned as he stretched his long legs. Getting up and sighing, he walked out the door. I didn't jump up and run upstairs to talk to my woman friends. What he said about me might make them feel jealous and angry again. I would feel awkward. Even though it was about mortal sin, I secretly relished the attention. It also scared me to the core; it was referring to sex that was way beyond my library stack behavior.

I struggled with my internal conflicts, the thrill of sexual attention, and the need to consider myself sexually responsible. My attitude toward sexual activity was moving in a healthy direction compared to high school even if I was not 100% sure I knew my own answers to situations all of the time. It didn't occur to me that my growing bipolar energies were responsible for so much male attention. They could have been misread as sexual energy.

Physical activity played an important role in my high school years and in college. Dance absorbed much of the energy that causes sexual conflict for many young adults. I was able to keep my physical energy under control with so many emotional conflicts. During freshman year I had tried out for a dance group that performed at half time for the basketball games. My dance form was still like a ballerina's freshman year, and I did not adjust to the drill team look. I was not chosen, but I did not give up. I went to the games and watched the dance team at half time. By sophomore year I had thought through the type of dancing that I needed to make the team. I was extremely excited the night that I made the team, jumping up and down, well beyond those appropriate limits. While I no longer roomed with Frankie, she came to congratulate me and calm me down.

The motion of these practices each week and the performances relaxed my moods. Belonging to the group felt wonderful. We danced at NCAA tournaments on television. We went to New York City for the NIT and danced at the semi-finals. The manager of Madison Square Garden requested that we dance at the final game, even if our team didn't win. However, our team won and it was so sensational walking out on the basketball court where the teams had just played. TV cameras were whirling and focusing on us as we kicked our legs and marched to the music, a dance and drill military song.

However, on the bus ride back to college, I sat alone. I wondered and worried what was wrong with me. Pam had sat with me on the way out, having a great time. Sitting there on the thirteen-hour ride home, I wallowed in self-pity and a million self-depreciating reasons. I cried in the dark of night. I read during the daylight hours. None of my experiences were adding up. Using the developmental psychology that Dr. Ann had taught me, I reviewed the areas of my life where I was doing well. Everything checked out okay except my friendships with other women.

Actually, when I got off the bus in New York City, I went into the hotel, and took off with my latest boyfriend, Mickey, until it was time for practice. I also went home to see my mom. I didn't spend anytime developing friendships with the women in the dance group during the outing to NYC. I went in my own direction. The bus ride home was merely a statement of fact regarding how I had spent my time and with whom I had bonded. I failed to grasp the obvious. Self-rejection was becoming a block against reality. My thought process was really distorted, but I denied it.

Back on campus, students were alive with social justice awareness. Parties spontaneously emerged after social justice meetings. Black and white students took the opportunities to meet and learn from each other. Dating patterns were reflected on campus, black and white couples dotting the walkways down from the dormitory, down the hill past the tennis courts, and into the student union.

At one of these parties, I danced with Wally, a new black friend. He was of medium height, a trim football player with a guarded smile. We planned our first date for the next weekend; we were both obviously nervous. We went to a party and someone stole my purse. Wally searched the whole house though until he found it.

Worried that someone did it because we were an interracial couple, I appreciated his protective and responsible nature where my welfare was concerned. In the country at large, people were just opening their eyes to the fact that racial prejudice was doing all of us an injustice. Hatred toward an interracial couple like us that evening was hopefully going to melt in all of the education that was happening in regard to equality. However, that night my stolen purse was cause for worry about the reality of hatred.

We dated from the end of sophomore year through junior year, getting to know each other's background and going out with friends. Many students commented that Wally was so much easier to be with than other blacks on campus because he spoke with a white man's accent. Many of the other black students spoke with a black accent or a Creole language. Wally went to a white high school and rarely spoke with a black accent around those on campus.

Who is he, students would ask. He was a leader whose mind we couldn't see working except by the results. Wally brought divergent people comfortably closer to each other. He helped the freshman black men to get involved on campus.

If a young man confronted me as to why I was dating a black guy, Wally's anger would rise. One night outside a party, he had a fistfight with one such ignorant student. After he first safely tucked me in the car, I could hear them insulting each other through the windows. Fists cracked jawbones and hit stomachs. When the two fighters had enough, Wally got in behind the wheel of the car.

"Are you alright?" I asked with fear in my voice.

"Sort of. I worry how we can go through life together when these brawls can happen because of our friendship," he said as he dropped his head on the steering wheel.

Indeed, we had even talked about marriage. He had a full scholarship to Harvard Law School, but it conflicted with his true mission. He really wanted to establish a private high school in a major city to help his own people. As it was, he would be late picking me up for a date, because he was in the dorm-helping freshman. They were scared to death to leave their rooms or even go to class on a 98% white campus. On my side, I wanted to be able to teach and do it in peace. Moving to Cambridge so I would be safe in an ivory tower apartment did not fit my personality or Wally's. The final, sad decision was to go our own ways. It turned out to be a good decision. We had learned a lot about life and multiculturalism. I learned that no can be a very loving choice.

I wanted to go and get away from the hurt and tears of our decision. Backpacking in Europe was my choice. My mom said absolutely not; it's not a proper way for a young lady to travel. I could choose an educational tour with supervision. I signed up for a theology/ philosophy tour to twelve universities in Germany, Austria, Switzerland, and Holland.

The tour left the end of junior year. I wallowed in my sad feelings, with an unhappy face for most of the trip. The young men on the trip left me alone except for Danny who tried to cheer me up. I spent more time with the women and didn't feel left out.

We met at Kennedy International Airport in New York, excited until the delays were announced. Six hours beyond our estimated time of departure, we boarded the aircraft. We flew across the ocean to Reykjavik, Iceland in a propjet. Looking out the window, I gasped because one propeller was not turning. We landed safely in grey overcast weather. Once inside the air terminal, peering out the airport window to our plane, we had a close view of the ground crew removing our damaged engine. Three hours later, we saw the men carry a new engine across the airfield and lunge it into our aircraft.

We boarded nervously but were immediately treated to a wonderful fish dinner while looking over the Northern Atlantic waters. The stewardesses were proper and congenial. They wore blue uniforms with straight skirts and flight pins on their skycaps. They tried their best to make up for the delay. We landed in Luxemburg, thinking that it was time for a well-deserved rest. Instead, Reverend Karl, our fearless leader, announced in his piercing loud voice that we were now going to board a train for the Volkswagen plant in Germany. Straining to understand the priest's need to drive us, we climbed into the train with all of our belongings. One student said that we were behind schedule to pick up our Volkswagens at the factory. Upon arrival near the factory, Reverend Karl allowed us to sleep six hours before we gathered for the first review of our academic work.

We purchased our five Volkswagens and rode toward Berlin via the Autobahn. At the entrance to the Autobahn, we had to be checked in at the guard gate on the West German side. They exchanged our license plates for East German visitor's plates. We were studying inside the cars, and I changed cars at one point. We saw the police motoring on the side roads throughout our trip. The terrain was simply beautiful. The plains of the North German Lowland were dotted with lakes, moors, marshes, meadows, pastures and small towns. At one point we climbed out of our car and watched East German's flying home made planes. We starred at each other. We were living worlds apart with the results of World War II between us. No smiles passed over our faces; however, we exchanged nods of acceptance before we climbed back into the car.

The northern part of Germany is known as Prussia – a land with its own geographic, cultural, and historical identity. We were privileged to see Germany on the Audubon from many aspects that day. I had tension in my arms and breath was slow as I scanned the countryside and its obvious presence of police, guards, gates, and guns. Terrain still held hostage by destruction frightened us and reminded us about faith in God.

We arrived at the Berlin border. East Germany was the socialist state established in 1949 in the Soviet zone of occupied Germany as well as the East Berlin portion of the allied-occupied capital city. However, was reunited with West Germany in 1990 and is now a part of Germany. In 1969 the Berlin wall was still in place. Because I had changed cars, guards at the entrance to the city made the car in front of us wait for me. We had to get back in our original cars before they checked our passports and changed our license plates. Some cars were searched. It was cultural eeriness for this American.

Fences and minefields protected West Berlin from East Germany. We drove along the abyss to suburbia where we stayed in an attractive set of apartments. We were treated to a delicious meal at the huge beautiful home of the reverend's friends. Conversation that evening about concentration camps was to be championed by spine tingling moments when we took a trip to Dachau a few weeks later. Much of the education during that trip was outside the classroom.

After our long journey to Berlin, we drove over to the University of Berlin to start the long awaited dialogues with German theology students. Each session boasted a predetermined subject for dialogue. For example, we discussed the death of God debate and Vatican II with its ramifications for change and ecumenical dialogue. The socializing afterwards in bars and restaurants really greased the conversations. The students voiced a concern that was repeated throughout the trip. America could make the same mistakes with black people as they had made with the Jewish race. I blinked at the irony and never pinned them down. Questions twisted inside of me with anxiety and timidity. What had they learned from the anti-Semitism? The responses might have shed some light on their viewpoints, but my emotions blocked that chance.

My head was on a pivot because of the unexpected views of the students we met at each whistle-stop. Stereotypes were blown away, leaving room for my twenty-year-old brain to accommodate and assimilate new thinking. I enjoyed the landscape of Bavaria, the Alps of Switzerland, Austria and the flat country of Holland. I felt an intense absorption in the professors' lectures. A small cultural gesture emerged after the lectures as the students rapped their knuckles on their desks in approval as we might clap. It was one of many small ways to enter another culture. I rapped.

One classmate had relatives living in the mountains above Frankfort that he had never met. Eight of us drove up on a free weekend. The sun was setting over the farm fields and mountains when the grandma and grandpa warmly greeted us in front of the main house. They had us drive to the front door of almost new hunting quarters. We didn't unpack before being escorted into a restaurant on the farm grounds. Beer and wine flowed freely for hours as we danced and dined to an according player. Most of us begged off more beer by saying nix and holding a hand or two over the top of the beer stein. Some classmates went outside, quite lit, and ran across the fields, hand in hand.

The next morning grandpa invited us with non-verbal gestures to come to breakfast in the main house. We sat at a long table while grandma, always smiling, cut pieces of fresh round bread that she held on her chest. Plates of goose liver were offered followed by cherry brand in exquisite little crystal glasses. These people were surly excited about seeing us.

The moment of explanation for their elation came as we were asked to climb into a bus and go to the graveyard on the side of their mountain. We arrived and glanced at the exquisite view of farm fields and distant mountains captured in the sunshine. One relative who spoke English finally broke the mystery and told us the story. Grandma and grandpa's son was buried in one of a line of graves of German soldiers. He had prayed and waited for the Americans to come and liberate him and his country. Stunned, I thought about how Jesus comes in our weaknesses, not our strengths. The simple statement about not judging – let God be God – belonged on his grave. Was he too weak to leave Hitler's army? Not intelligent enough? Did he feel trapped? Was he a simple soul?

Grandma started to cry and tried to speak to us. Our translator said that her son waited for the Americans who did not come before his death. She wanted us to know that we were the first Americans to come to the farm since the war. She celebrated with us and thanked us for letting her son know that Germany was free. The weekend was the biggest theological discussion of the trip. I rapped my knuckles on his gravestone.

My fears of German police subsided as I came to terms with my own problems. By the end of the trip, I was more open to my male classmates. The excitement of seven weeks in Europe helped my integration. Memories created gave me strength for my own journey. My mind had incorporated many new venues.

CHAPTER FOUR

Senior Year (1969-1970)

The last autumn of my beloved college days arrived far too early. Feminist air filled my lungs while in Europe and followed me to the university. Equality with men in Europe had left me as a cross between a hippy and an independent woman. I landed ready to travel into the semester with renewed sightings of freedom. I returned to university living with five housemates in a terrific off-campus home. My goals were for having male friends, teaching, and completing my college courses for graduation. I had finished my student teaching in my advanced teaching program of junior year. Thus I qualified to substitute teach in the city school system and make some money.

The semester started off as I planned. Dating boys coincided with various needs. Some came to cook dinner for me and my housemates, eat a free meal, and relieve me of my culinary duties. I had dates with other young men who knew where the parties were taking place. Sometimes my dates talked to each other in front of our house. They met each other coming and going, picking me up or bring a pot or pan for making our dinner.

One afternoon, I strolled home from classes on campus under an umbrella of autumn leaves that were still clinging to September's trees in crimson colors, shades of gold, and some lingering greenery. I skipped onto our stone front steps, crossed the porch, and opened the door. Before I could put my books down on the dining room table, I was greeted by two of my housemates, Frankie and Celina.

"Can we have a moment of your busy time in the living room?" they asked.

"Yes," I agreed, as I noticed the tension mounting.

"What are you doing, Fizzer?" Frankie inquired with looks of grave concern.

"The boys are meeting you coming and going in front of the house. You have a pile of phone messages from boys out of state that need to be answered," Frankie continued. A sad aura descended over the living room.

"Are you jealous?" I shot back.

"Heavens, no, we are engaged," Celina said. They dropped their heads and rubbed their engagement rings to make them sparkle.

They left me alone and said no more that day. I fell back into the green pillows of the soft sofa accenting my tense muscles. Anger rose in my chest. I wasn't sleeping around. I made my bed upstairs every morning and there were no wrinkled sheets until I climbed in alone at midnight or one o'clock in the morning. Tears threatened to trickle down my cheeks, but my tense body would not let a drop transverse my face.

I was twenty years old and had no understanding that the manic-depressive disease in my body was increasing. I was to have a breakdown at twenty-six, a frequently occurring time for the disease to appear in individuals' lives. An enormous amount of energy of various kinds traversed my being on an upward spiral. A few deep breaths led me to some conclusions. Men were my priority; Frankie and Celina had a lot more women friends than I ever amassed. Women didn't like me that much, and I liked intelligent male students. They didn't limit my abilities, perceptions, or attempts at equality of friendship. I had no reason to trade in my constellation of friends for a secure ring circling my finger. I kept sex at a safe distance. My international appreciation of sexual equality had turned my manic head forever – at least this semester.

Women suffered from sexual stigma in 1969, especially in regard to the work force. The professional choices still mostly ranged from teacher to nurse to secretary or homemaker. I decided that teaching had the most chances for creativity. Then I decided to add a constellation of male friends to my graduation plans. Women of my time were beginning to develop self-confidence similar to men growing up in our culture, especially in a college-educated population. The fact that I spent more time with men than women during my college years was valuable but was to produce some alarming results.

Few if any students lived together in the 1960's. Marriage was still the accepted and expected norm, at least among the Catholic population. Five young men proposed to me over the span of the first few months of my senior year. Sometimes I gasped for breath because I had thought of them as friends.

One night I said a painful no to Jerome's proposal of marriage over a long distance phone call. We belonged to the Catholic parish youth group back home with Reverend Mickey. Jerome and I were idealistic philosophers who hung out together in the coffee houses around town. I saw us as 1960's Woodstock revolutionaries out to change the world. I did not think about marriage at all. One summer he invited me to his parents' summer cottage in the mountains. One night he rowed us out into the middle of the lake with the moon shining. He told me that he thought about being alone with me like this all of the time. I couldn't wait to get out of the boat, away from him, and the whole scene.

Tim traveled from another university to speak with me about marriage. The night he came to see me, he showed up in my living room and waited past midnight for me to come home. He said that I was the only woman he considered worthy of marriage. I remember crying and stroking the top of his head as I said I didn't agree. I slowly walked upstairs waving good-bye. Steve was starting to hint about what we'd do together after graduation. I had to put him off, as I couldn't stand the emotional pain of breaking one more relationship. Wally was dating someone who loved and understood him very well, so we stayed away from each other. I was truly amazed that most of the young men didn't see things my way. They were my buddies, my friends. I honestly thought that they were ruining a good thing.

My housemates decided that they had a solution to my problematic behavior. Chuck had lost his apartment and had no place to live during the first semester senior year. While I was on campus attending classes one day, Chuck was offered the extra bed in my bedroom while my regular roommate was on an outdoor education program for eight weeks. I was furious when I came home and went upstairs to find Chuck's luggage all over my room. I stood in the hallway looking in with frozen silence. I wondered if I had lost my ability to control anything. I leaned against the wall feeling dizzy, woozy. The room appeared to be torn apart in jarring angles. I hopped inside as I heard heavy footsteps on the stairs. I swirled around in a circle just grabbing onto a dresser drawer. When he stepped over the threshold, I starred at his magnificent, handsome appearance. He was of medium height and build with large chocolate eyes, a long nose, wide smile, and sandy blond hair. Taking deep breaths I attempted speech.

"What are you doing here?" I almost squeaked out of my lungs.

"Roomie," he said with a beautiful smile and long outstretched arms.

"Why?" I asked with frustration.

"I need a place to stay for a couple of months," he replied.

"A few months," I gasped in horror. He merely smiled another enigmatic smile.

That night I figured out how to prepare for bed. I had to take all my nightclothes into the bathroom, hoping he didn't interrupt my bath. Or was I honestly hoping that he would? I came out wrapped in a terry cloth robe and slippers. I walked into my room, rather our room, and became dizzy once again. I saw jarring lights in my mind, not the soothing Northern Lights I looked for inside my mind ever since Mr. Class pointed them out in the winter skies at home. When I opened my eyes I saw Chuck bending over an umbrella at the end of his bed. He turned around and saw me standing in the room.

"Oh," he said.

"Excuse me," he continued.

"I am putting up my umbrella for some privacy. I'm a single guy, you know."

I was humiliated. Did he think I was a wild woman? Me, scrupulous me? Instead of speaking, I stalked out of the room. When I had composed myself, I walked back into the room, heading straight for my own bed. I decided not to talk with any of my housemates about the incident because I was furious with them for this nonsensical arrangement. Pulling the covers over my head, I starred out the window into the night air. This window had already become my escape from life in general. I watched the city buses go by and said my prayers of thankfulness. Now I fell asleep forgetting to be thankful.

"Good night, roomie," he shot across the abyss we shared.

I ignored him, waiting for my anger to slow down. Whether or not I was ready for more of Chuck's attentions, he became my bodyguard. I was in his care everywhere. He had a car and drove me to my substitute teaching assignments and around the city for shopping. He was always with me on campus in the snack bar or waiting for me after class. I had a small respite when he had his own classes to attend.

On one of these afternoons, I went to the snack bar by myself. I was talking to three boys, John, I already knew, and two of his friends. I had just met them when Chuck rushed in a side door and literally slid next to me.

"Hi, I'm Trisha's roommate," he introduced himself to the three gentlemen.

"Good-bye, Trisha," said John as they all left smiling.

"I demand an explanation," I said with a red and angry face. Once again Chuck had intruded upon my life and attempts to make friends.

"You truly embarrassed me, Chuck. You make me feel like a loose woman. I'm not and I'm hurt," I said.

"Stick with me," was all he said with a smile.

Polarized

"Have Fizzer (my nickname) in by 11:00 tonight because I want to get some sleep," he'd say as he greeted my date at the front door. He'd shake their hand as I left.

Soon everyone in our group of friends and acquaintances were aware that I had a male roommate. I laughed often because it made me so nervous. I was also panicking because my supply of dates was beginning to dry up. I didn't need any protection. I just liked dating because it was so much fun. It suited my energy level and I was comfortable with the way I viewed myself.

The full story had other components besides how I acted out my strong energy level. Growing up in a mostly female household, I wanted balance in my understanding of the opposite sex. However, I was still slapping boys who were too affectionate and literally pushing tongues back in place. Morally, they caused me to become too aroused. Also, coming upstairs, Chuck was waiting for me in his bed across the room.

"I saw you on the front porch, Fizzer," began Chuck's typical conversation. He would then proceed to review his objections to that evening's date. The only young man Chuck approved of was Richard Frisch. Chuck was taking a course in marriage and family life. He had a mission and it was becoming obvious that I was his practice target. Richard was handsome, stabile, owner of a huge smile and quiet ways. He was my age, a senior classmate. We had met freshman year, and I didn't think that he noticed me.

"Oh, well," I said in regard to my fast paced, freshman life at that time. Like a child at play, I raced to the next dance, the next class, and the next new person to meet. I ran into him only because we had mutual friends in a large group. Off and on we did chitchat in that group, but we never dated. Then came senior year.

After my return from Europe, I was already facing a tumultuous senior year. One Friday night in September our household had a party. Someone inevitably spilled beer on the kitchen floor. Rushing into the house from another party, running into the kitchen, sliding through spilled beer, I landed squarely in front of Richard. I thought to myself,

"Oh, I forgot about him."

As we started to talk, he handed me a beer.

"Let's go," he said with a crisp determination I was to come to know well.

There were many parties that Friday night. We walked around laughing and talking together. We saw each other everyday. We rode around in his convertible looking at houses. He liked brick and I liked clapboard siding. I thought to myself, not a chance of marriage with such differences. He always had a twenty-dollar bill in his wallet.

"I can hardly believe you run around, even downtown to substitute teach, with only one or two dollars in your pocket. You don't take very good care of yourself, Trisha," Richard stated one day while driving around.

Richard curbed my bad habits acquired as a college student. One evening when he came to pick me up for a date, I had had a lot of wine while playing cards in the dining room.

"Oh, oh, I'm late," I said as I raced upstairs to change clothes. I had trouble opening a drawer in my semi-drunken state. I pulled, I tugged, and it came flying out. I jumped aside as it dropped to the floor. Downstairs my housemates had just let Richard in the front door. They told him I was upstairs getting ready as the loud crash rang down the staircase. I rushed into the bathroom splashing water on my face. I said an act of contrition, hoping for forgiveness. I walked downstairs and apologized to him.

Whatever Richard liked about me, he was getting my attention. He was matter of fact that he already had a firm interest in me. I wondered if it was the clothes I wore, my jewelry, what I cooked, or my interest in theology. He listened like he was enamored of everything I did. He had a peaceful sway over me that was mesmerizing.

Richard came to our house one evening in a blue mohair sweater and asked me to sit in the living room. He told me that he really liked the fact that I was going to be a professional woman. He thought that I was sexy and beautiful. We could have children together after the marriage.

"I'll give you three weeks to answer my proposal," he said. I said that I would consider his offer of marriage.

"Oh, that's wonderful," he stated with a warm smile.

"I'll be back in three weeks," he said. I was not very interested in his business courses. I never have had a good business mind, but I respected what interested him. I was mainly taken by his peaceful ways and my serene feelings around him. It was not only my emotional base calming down, but I was also starting to develop an organized lifestyle. I had to in order to be on time for our dates. At first I was never ready because of my eternal card playing and wine drinking in our dining room. He kindly got the point across that if we were going out, he wanted me to be ready. I was embarrassed, of course, and I was ready. I missed playing cards.

My thought process was influenced by his methodical mind. He set boundaries and limits and I ate them up like candy. His proposal of marriage was the most attractive and alluring among the five proposals I received. His request seemed like he was taking care of himself. The other boys were all emotion and few plans.

Hanging out with Richard, I was thinking clearer and making more money as a substitute teacher. I was getting along with my housemates as I had more in common with them than when I was dating two or three boys on the same day. I was tired of Chuck being my roommate, as nice as he was. I wanted him to find an apartment and leave. I had all the necessary messages I needed from brother Chuck.

My feelings for Richard were a combination of peace and romance. Missing was the Scarlet O'Hara and Rhett Butler high drama and romantic swings involved in dating and saying no to the other marriage proposals. Sometimes I worried about the lack of excitement because the emotions should be everything. This time he was everything.

He came to see me three weeks later, and I accepted his offer of marriage. I was sitting on the same sofa where Frankie and Celina tried to tell me that I was out of control.

"Have you thought over my proposal?" he asked.

"Yes I have," I said a little nervously.

"Yes, yes I want to marry you," I said and put aside my anxiety. He wore a light blue mohair sweater and dark slacks. I remember his chocolate eyes watching me with anticipation as I slowly gave my answer.

"That's wonderful," he smiled.

He started to make his methodical plans. He would find a part-time job and buy me a ring. He said that he would save his money and when he could afford to, we would be officially engaged. I was of the school that we should start to celebrate right away. Champagne, parties, and new clothes for my new image were on my calendar of events.

He also knew how to wait. My frustration level was rising. He took me to nice places as well as long study sessions in his home across town. His housemates did a lot of studying, too. He found a position installing fire equipment. The atmosphere in my household quieted down. No more boys coming to date me, and none of Richard's friends were planted in the living room to watch Chuck say goodnight to my dates.

Before the last night as roommates, Chuck took me into his confidence. He was going into the seminary to become a priest after graduation. I sat bold upright in bed holding a muffled scream inside my hands.

"That's wonderful, Chuck. Congratulations," I said.

"Thanks, Fizzer, I really wanted you to know before we finished being roommates."

Shaking inside, I hid my sarcasm. A good little Catholic girl had roomed with a Catholic priest in the making. We had not had sex or even dated; rather, he was practicing his marriage and family skills, warming up for his ministry. Still, my rigid background had trouble assimilating my relationship with Chuck.

One afternoon when I was coming out of a lab in the science building, I saw Richard coming up the stairs beneath the large pendulum that swung in front of glass windows. His face was beat red with anger.

"What's the matter?" I said. "My parents do not want us to get married," he said. "They have never even met me," I squealed. He said,

"They want us to come home for Thanksgiving. They will talk to us."

When we arrived on Wednesday, Thanksgiving felt to me like a powder cage of anxiety. On Thanksgiving I wore the most exciting pumpkin dress and sling back shoes I had ever owned. I had my hair swept up in the front and long in the back. I felt beautiful. We were to wait until Sunday night when we would go to a concert that his dad was playing in his orchestra. Then we would go out for a sandwich and the restaurant caucus. Richard and I twisted our fingers under the restaurant table as we talked. Everything seemed to go well. We went back to school.

A few weeks later, Richard's dad was in New York City playing a concert. He called my mom.

"Richard and Trisha are too young to marry," he said.

"With young people starting to live together, I admire Richard and Trisha for wanting to get married," she replied. I have since thought that controlling others is a lack of attention to ourselves. God does not make us to control others; we are made to cooperate with God in controlling ourselves. His parents dropped their objections.

Richard made enough money to buy me a ring. On a Friday afternoon in March, I rushed into my house to show my housemates the graduation ring I just finished paying for at the campus bookstore. My housemates exchanged alarmed glances. Someone squeaked,

"Your ring?" Rushing to dress for dinner with Richard for his birthday, I missed their voice intonations. One housemate told me that my ring looked clunky with my soft dress. She ordered me to wear my school ring during the day.

Richard picked me up and we headed downtown. We went to a really sophisticated restaurant, one of the best in town. We had steaks and scotch sours. After large pieces of chocolate cake, we strolled leisurely toward the parking garage. Richard opened the door of the car for me. Then he went around the back of the car and threw up the trunk of the car. He slid behind the wheel of the car with a little box. He gave it to me and I popped it open. It was a gorgeous diamond ring. I gasped in surprise and excitement.

When we left the parking garage, I thought he was taking me home.

"No," he said.

"I'm taking you to the apartments where Chuck is living," he added.

"Are they having a party for us?" I asked.

"Oh, no!" he replied.

"Oh yes!" I tried again.

We arrived at the door with the ring on my finger. Richard opened the door.

"Surprise," everyone yelled. It was a wonderful party. One of our friends sent a telegram that said this diamond would be a symbol of something beautiful. I was exuberant.

CHAPTER FIVE

Marriage (1970-1974)

My mom made a drastic change in her lifestyle when Kathleen left for the university. She sought to fill her empty nest syndrome with a move to Naples, Florida. She needed a fresh start in life after raising her family alone. Norm and Eileen Berk were living in a complex of condominiums they had built with a view of the Gulf of Mexico. Mom purchased one of their condos. After graduation, I moved into mom's two-bedroom condominium. The location was similar to any advertisement for living in the Caribbean. The newness of her home was surrounded by lush vegetation and a swimming pool right outside of her porch. My old sailboat was anchored down by the chickee, a roof made of palm fronds to cover a fishing dock. I could walk to the beach right across a small bridge. Back then we had a sweeping vista of the gulf without today's built high-rise apartments.

One evening before she left our original home, we sat together on the living room sofa having a cup of tea. We were drawing up plans for my wedding in NYC. We would have a small reception at the Plaza Hotel. When she decided to move to Naples, she never said anything about those wedding plans again. She did tell us that she had no feeling for leaving her home of twenty plus years. She simply packed the van and left. Her emotional blocking included that night when we shared cups of tea and wedding dreams. I never asked her where the wedding plans had gone? I had the same ability to block emotionally painful topics. She needed a fresh start in life after raising her family alone.

Obviously, the wedding plans had to be rearranged. Once I was living there, we tried to figure out the best modus operandi. The wedding plans turned out to be fairly complex. We would wed in upstate NY, where close family was living. It was geographically the most convenient for family and friends.

That summer before the wedding, I worked as a waitress in a pancake house. It was fun and afforded me the money to purchase Richard a gold wedding band that matched my band. Richard visited me once in Naples, and we went out a lot together. I knew I was in love, and besides, I was tired of being in close quarters with mom. Every time I received a phone call from Richard, she would come in the room and listen. If I was in the kitchen and on the phone with Richard, she had to come racing in to clean a spot off of her dress. I was ready to move on and give mom the space she needed for her new life.

After Richard left, the wedding preparations went on and on. I made dresses for the honeymoon. There was a party across the way in the Berk's complex. Norm, Eileen, and Grandma Ceil had caught a great number of specialty fish called snook and froze them for a party in my honor. It was a very special gesture in part because snook is a delicacy only caught legally in August and September. I remember crying tears of joy as dinner was served. I didn't know I mattered so much to my friends.

I continued to work to earn money for my wedding needs. Mom and Grandma Ceil, the Berks' grandmother, rode with mom to pick me up at the pancake house. They laughed that Ceil was riding shotgun so my mom would be safe. We would go to our friend's house, and I'd tell stories about the people in the restaurant to make everyone laugh. I relished being the center of attention.

In the beginning of August, right before I was to leave to go to upstate NY where the wedding was to take place, I was sitting in our living room counting my tips from the Pancake House. I was smoking cigarettes, one after another. Mom came in and sat down. She proceeded to tell me about every girl we knew growing up who was actually pregnant on her wedding day. I was listening with both ears for a while because I never knew about some of these pregnancies. Then she popped the question.

"Are you pregnant? I want to know with all of the money that is being spent," she said.

"No," I snapped. I was thoroughly humiliated.

She didn't know about the book Richard had given me when he was visiting. I hid it since she was becoming so intrusive. He said it would help me understand what he wanted to do on the honeymoon. I thanked him for the book. I was really nervous about entering a lifetime sexual commitment even though we were attracted to each other. Books of this nature can go only so far in fostering understanding. I threw the book out. Our experiences of each other turned out to be the real teachers.

When it was time to pack, I placed all of my souvenirs in the same suitcase. Only one or two were from Wally. They were works of art, so I thought to myself that I could always remember him as a friend. Why can't I have a friend to remember even if I was about to marry Richard? I popped them in the suitcase and closed it up.

Mom and I traveled from Naples, through Kennedy Airport, NY to upstate New York. My plane was late arriving in New York and I had to dash through the airport holding the white silk and lace wedding dress above my head, from gate to gate. My suitcase of memoirs was the only one lost on the long trip.

Richard and I had to speak with Father Burkite, the priest who was to marry us. Because it was not our regular parish, Father Burkite was really doing us a favor. My brother-in-law was going to play the *Ave Maria* with his violin. The priest liked that idea. Then he showed the plan for the rest of the Mass. He wanted me to process in to the *Gaelic Hymn to the Blessed Mother*, one of his favorites. I was also Irish and so it would fit together very well. *Ode to Joy*, played on the organ, was my selection for a recessional. I took his other suggestions and politely declined the entrance hymn. He was agreeable and I breathed a sigh of relief. He was pretty nice, after all, and it was his church.

He took us on a tour of his very modern church. I was to place a rose at the feet of the statue of Mary. He said not many folks recognized her in the cone shaped funnel with a halo on the top, but he had placed it there for the young people. He had side altars for the elderly. Everyone had something that made the church his or hers.

My love of beauty was satisfied the day of our wedding. The bridesmaids' colors were fashionably green and blue with long paisley sashes. I had purchased my own dress on sale. It had long sleeves and was a little hot for August, but I looked beautiful. My maid of honor was Kathleen, and two sister-in-laws were the bridesmaids. I wanted to please the families, so I never spoke up for my desire to include my friends, Margo and Sarah as bridesmaids and have a big wedding party. Anxiety, fear, and lack of self esteem made it impossible to assert myself. For a lifetime I have regretted my weaknesses. For once in my life I really had exquisite thoughts about myself. Normally, I thought that I was at best plain. When growing up, I used to look in a mirrored light switch on the downstairs bathroom wall and tell mom that I didn't like my face.

She would say, "I wish I was as pretty as you are, Trisha. Stop saying that. Look at your beautiful eyes and your wavy brown hair. You are very pretty." I barely believed it. The exception was that one-day in August.

I was very nervous as I processed down the aisle on my brother's arm. My stomach cramped and I could taste the morning's orange juice. I reached Richard at the base of the altar.

"I feel sick," was all I said to my husband to be.

"You look beautiful," he said as he just smiled.

How can any man decide to marry a woman who would have his children, cook his meals, and make his bed? Not to mention, argue and make up with him? Did Richard realize what he was getting into?

During the Ave Maria, I managed to turn slightly and see my brother-in-law bow down on his violin. It is still in my memory bank as a beautiful gesture. After Mass and the wedding vows, we left the altar to Ode to Joy. The reception was fun at my family's apartment party room overlooking a swimming pool. Relatives and college friends were there. We danced on the carpeted floors and had a great lunch. It went too fast. I threw my bouquet and my old roommate from senior year, who spent so much time at outdoor education camp, caught it. We ran out the door waving good-bye.

We honeymooned in Canada and had a good time together. Friends said it was best to wait six months for the honeymoon until you were adjusted to each other, but we were in love. Couples living together before the wedding day was not the custom. We were happy enough to honeymoon right away.

Then we drove to the home of Richard's parents. They had a second reception for us. I was very nervous, yet anxiety had activated on a daily basis from the day I left Naples, Florida to marry Richard. We packed up the presents that we could take with us and drove into the southeast. Richard was about to begin his two-year commitment as a lieutenant in the U.S. Army during the Vietnam War. ROTC in college added a great deal to his growth and development. He was the ROTC Band leader and serving his country was important to him. The army was the arena for him to strike out toward adulthood. I was a peace person, a child of the sixties, and a semi-hippie kind of liberal thinker. Before the wedding, we had already resolved our differences concerning the army and the Vietnam War.

For when the draft came into existence, we were seniors in college. Richard's number was low on the list. This meant his chances of being drafted into the army and going to Vietnam were very insignificant. I was excited; Richard was upset that he might miss his chance to go into the army and support his country. He was emotionally upset the day he told me his decision, and it was unusual for him to lose his peace. However, we were ready on our wedding day to go forward with some understanding about what we were facing. My compromise thinking was that Richard believed in what he was doing and I supported him. I would pray for the Vietnam War to end before he was ever, ever sent overseas to possibly face death.

And so, we drove south while getting used to being one, not two. We arrived early for Richard to report for duty. At a real estate office near post, we introduced ourselves to a real estate agent. She was elderly, tall, and thin, with a silvery bun on top of her head.

"I'm Miss Brenda. Are you a lieutenant?" she inquired as she shook our hands.

"Yes. We are looking for a place to live for the next twelve weeks."

"Follow me," she said as she rattled some keys on her desk.

We went across town in her car. It was a long drive from the army post. She pulled up in front of an old southern mansion, replete with southern pillows.

"Here we are at the Dingledarling Plantation," she said with a grand sweep of her hand toward the stately home.

A gardener was mowing the front lawn. Richard and I starred in a state of shock. The apartments for officers near post looked dirty and infested with cockroaches. This mansion was awesome in comparison. We went inside to find a real mansion with 19th century furniture. On the second floor Miss Brenda opened the door to a large furnished apartment. High ceilings matched huge clean rooms. Despite the hour-long drive to post, we agreed to rent it for the length of our stay. It was a lovely nest for newly weds.

As an officer's wife, I was emotionally entwined with his duty because of the Vietnam War. The surreal living arrangements of the Dingledarling Plantation made it easier to endure the fears of war. Almost all of his classmates from Military Intelligence school went to Viet Nam and died. A speechless awareness came; Richard was still alive.

Miss Brenda told us that another officer and his wife lived next door to us upstairs.

"Are you a lieutenant?" Now we understood her mysterious question.

More light was shed on her desire for officers only as we returned downstairs. She opened the apartment on the first floor with another sweeping gesture. The fireplace we could see across the room was in her home, the owner of Dingledarling Plantation. Miss Brenda reminded me of a Nancy Drew character in mystery books that I read as a child.

Miss Brenda voluntarily sent her mammy up, a heavyset black woman replete with an apron and bare feet, to make new draperies and add a few homey touches to the living room and dining room. She contrasted drastically with college demonstrations.

My favorite spot in the kitchen was the pantry. When I would lift my dust mop, a pile of nuts would be nestled underneath. I could hear the squirrels running up and down the walls of the old house. I felt anxiety all of the time. I almost chain smoked cigarettes when Richard was in the fields on practice maneuvers for a few days.

I had to drive him to post whenever I used our convertible. Then I stayed on post to shop at the commissary or the PX, the Post Exchange. Food and goods were inexpensive. I'd always try to buy new spices as I thought that was the mark of a good cook. Anxiety finally stopped disrupting my insecure thought process when I picked him up in his officer's uniform. Despite my misgivings about the war, he did look handsome. I tried to please him as much as possible.

I would clean the house as if we were going to stay forever. I'd imagine where I would place new furniture. I tried new recipes even though I always used too much garlic. I never learned how to cook as mom always did it to keep her mind off of daddy.

I read books all day and smoked cigarettes or I'd walk outside. The officer's wife next door was cordial but she worked. The anxiety didn't abate. I stopped smoking and saved enough money to fly mom to see where I was living. Telling people about the mansion made the anxiety more bearable. It was storybook living.

One day I tried to take my conservative best self to an officers' wives club meeting. It was billed as, The History of Military Hats, 1800-1950, at 9:00 a.m. sharp. Very strong coffee and tea were served up in silver urns that looked like a wedding present I had received from Richard's grandparents. Promptly at 9:00, military time, we all sat in a semi-circle for the lecture on military hats. They were neatly displayed on wavy silk material. Stories of the officers who wore them into various battles continued for an hour and a half.

I was wired from the strong coffee on top of my anxiety. I was afraid the other women might notice my lack of interest. I thought to myself that there must be some meaning for a group of thirty women riveted to their chairs in rapt attention for a presentation on military hats. I stayed awake respecting others' viewpoints and interests. Nothing ventured equaled never knowing, but I placed limits on the officers' wives club meeting. I didn't attend any more meetings. I did see some of the women at the officers' country club dinners and dances where I was more relaxed. They talked in a military jargon. I just smiled because I never excelled in foreign languages.

At the end I counted the days to leave. I packed up, making sure we had enough photos of our first love nest. Thinking about the future helped. I would soon forget the anxiety and loneliness of military life and talk about the good parts, my anxiety would end, and I would find some friends at the next stop. Our choice of Dingledarling Plantation had left me isolated. The Northern Lights I might have expected to see in my mind the first few months of our marriage never transpired. Yet I felt sadness at leaving our first married home. I was very sure we wouldn't return. We never have.

Christmas in Richard's hometown meant being surrounded by familiar faces and lots of merriment. I shared my pictures and was often the center of attention. We moved to another new post. Richard's assignment was for six months. We had secured an apartment and Richard went to Military Intelligence school. Neighboring mills blew blue and red dust into our windows. It didn't matter because it was our home. We stayed up late on weekend nights making curtains together as if we were to live there forever. We rented furniture and turned the old apartment into our paradise.

This was the first stop where I could stay long enough to have a job. I secured a first grade teaching position in a school in the Baltimore area. It meant having a classroom full of children with reading difficulties. It was January and they were falling behind in their schoolwork. I was to bring them up to reading at grade level by June. It meant making tapes and organizing material for several hours at night. It became our first bone of contention, as Richard wanted my attention. He liked the fact that I had a paycheck but thought the effort was too much.

The students placed with me because of there difficulties were restless because of their failure. Some parents objected to the fact that the switch in teachers might mean their son or daughter was below standard. Sometimes the children's acting out was the most aggravating part of being a teacher.

I was given a lovely little pin at the end of the year when I had to leave and move to yet another post. I hated to leave. I was declared a success because every one of my little students passed into the second grade. I was elated to take the compliments with me. Teaching provided Northern Lights because my self-concept was nourished by my teaching experiences and accomplishment. However, the experience of learning new ways to cope with the students, day by day, brought the usual anxieties I had grown to accept.

We packed up and moved south this time. We were given a little house in the officers' section of the post. Happily we began our usual home building. The curtains fit from the last apartment. We furniture shopped to buy a kitchen table and chairs. This time we did not have to rent furniture because I made money teaching. We had a common backyard with the other houses. We purchased lawn chairs and a grill. We spent all day on Saturdays bushes and gardens with bricks. We planted flowers and bought equipment to cut the grass and trim the bushes. The neighbors told us that we were out of our minds for spending money on government property. We made friends this stop because we were staying a whole year.

By August, one year after our wedding, we had another reason for our love of the home place. We were going to have a baby. The initial joy gave way quickly to simple realities of pregnancy. Richard brought home a bottle of champagne, which I immediately threw up. Apparently I had to consider what the baby was willing to tolerate.

I went to my Ob-Gyn. He was like a reassuring grandpa, soft spoken and gentle. He always smiled kindly and I would leave feeling less anxious. I stopped at my friend Mary's house on the way home. She had a new baby girl and was very maternal. She had a book with pictures of babies in the mother's uterus.

"Look, this is how old your baby is," she said.

I grabbed my stomach, rushed to the bathroom, and threw up. She was perplexed. She thought that the pictures of my five-month-old baby were marvelous. I was trying to accept that I had that baby inside of me. I had to accept that my friend thought less of me. I doubled my efforts to enjoy what she and the other new mother's were feeling so good about. I wanted my baby. I just wanted to see him when he came out.

I got that chance in April. My mother and my mother-in-law had a mission to keep me at home. I was sure he'd be okay because I had really taken care of myself. I had not taken a first grade position for more students with reading problems. They won, and we discovered that we had the ability to do so even if we had less money.

The baby was healthy at birth. In one week we found out that Richard's orders would be extended. Vietnam was heating up again and the army decided to retain outgoing 1st lieutenants. If we were out in two days we could go. Otherwise he was to stay in with a growing possibility of going to war. We had just become parents and protecting our child was on our minds and hearts.

The day we moved was scary but my adrenaline was running to complete the task of moving off post. We put our emotions on the back burner and moved with all our energies going in a positive direction. Richard was only one of a few from his original Military Intelligence class not on duty in Vietnam. We knew by now that the others had died. We were beyond speaking about it very much; we had a choice and he had served. We made our decision to try the impossible, and cleared post in forty-eight hours.

My neighbor was a pediatrician. She took our baby while we cleaned and packed. We looked like a *Saturday Evening Post* magazine: a young boy was mowing the lawn under the moving truck. We had to edge gardens and clean grease under each burner on the stove. We took our baby back from our neighbor, cleaned all of the blinds, and finished at three a.m. Neighbors had found an open home for us to stay in down the street for a week. We crept down the block carrying a bowl with a few left over eggs. We dropped into bed exhausted, achy, and sweaty. The next day we nervously awaited the army inspector. He passed us.

We had the baby baptized in a quiet, private ceremony in the army chapel. We didn't want to travel to Pennsylvania without the baptism. It was a relief to stand in the nave of the large stone chapel. A new born baby was wrapped in a hand made blanket that great grandma had knit for our first child.

I hardly remember pulling away. We had made some good friends. We had loved our home. Best of all, we had the bundle wrapped in a blanket, baptized and ready for travel. The relatives waiting for us said we reminded them of Jesus, Joseph, and Mary. Arriving at Richard's parents, he got out of the car, took the bundle out of my arms, walked down the street, and handed the baby to grandma. It was a moment of amazing grace.

We accepted grandma and grandpa's hospitality for three weeks while Richard's job-hunting expedition continued. He was taking interviews. I was taking care of my baby under grandma's watchful eyes. I was nursing, and that was frowned upon on the ground floor by grandma because she thought it to be a private activity.

"Give that baby a bottle," grandma would call upstairs.

"Come downstairs so I can play with my grandchild."

Generations of differences clashed and nothing could be done about it for those three weeks. The dicotomony between their generosity in allowing us to be housed in their home and some lack of comfortableness had to be compromised for the sake of harmony. Soon we were in our own home.

Richard accepted a good position in an Atlantic coastal city. Both of us were relieved for different reasons. Off we went with our packed trailer once again. He had already found an apartment that was large and airy. I met other teachers who were staying at home to raise their babies. Some had part time jobs and I eventually role-modeled them. When my child was ready for pre-school, I became an assistant. I enjoyed our home life and my work. The only negative situation was volunteering to teach a second grade communion class at our Catholic parish. The other teachers were not especially welcoming and I felt isolated.

Intertwined with the overall happiness we created for ourselves, I smoked to cure my ongoing anxiety. I thought it was from all of the moving around in new and unfamiliar situations. I smoked the most when I made clothes for myself or for the baby. I always felt like my ambition was being puffed out of the cigarette. I had too much energy was my thought. In retrospect, I was manic. I needed to be challenged in other ways. Sewing dresses and coats is very detailed work that requires focus, not the hurtful swells of manic behavior.

The power to concentrate on the garment took all of my energy and enjoyment. The driving goal was to see the final product, not to relax with the process. I did not relax with the joy of creating in the present moment. Also, if I was writing, a lack of integrating thoughts and emotions came into operation. If I were writing a sentence, I was missing a verb. The next sentence was missing a noun or adjective. It takes time to slow down and allow each part of a sentence to slide into place, creating harmony in the piece of work. Slowing down only gave me a view of my lack of self-confidence.

At the end of the two and one-half years we were in New Jersey, we still played tennis on Saturday mornings in a quiet, quaint town that was near our apartment. We would split an 8-cent soda after playing. Some days we would skip this luxury because we were saving to buy a home. Many of our teacher friends were moving away into their first homes. We would visit their new abodes. We wanted a home so badly that we sacrificed everything we could to stretch our budget. However, we were about three years younger than most of our friends. They had already gone through the saving process. Oh, we would drive around nice housing areas and drool.

Another motivating factor for relocating was the new prostitute ring that moved in next store. Also there was a prostitute across the street. Johns would ring my bell. I had to tell them that they had the wrong address. It was hard to take the baby outside alone. One night the prostitute ring next door was raided. Mattress after mattress was thrown out the back door. Drug dealers were invading the neighborhood, too. It was a bad time for a pretty apartment complex.

Richard's job-hunting turned up something of interest further north. I cried that I didn't want to leave my friends and my own work. It took so much time and energy to build a new home over and over. I had felt the most emotionally stable with my friends and surroundings, despite the growing problems in our apartment complex. We were moving against my will.

I discovered the reasons I cried so much about leaving. I was pregnant with our second child. I was very happy, but I was also a little worried about the move. I had stayed put for the first child, not even working. Stress can play havoc with any adult; however, experience teaches a pregnant adult to be careful. My priority had to be this second child. Somehow I had to protect my baby.

Our friends gave us a goodbye party and a Lenox vase to remember them. I never saw them again, and a long time elapsed before we found comfortable friends. I was in despair remembering them because relationships do not pop up in one's life like spring's flowers. I was also learning quite a bit about human nature and not grabbing the first friendly conversation to be a forever friend. We packed our trailer and drove northward.

We had a pretty apartment on the ground floor in the suburbs. Our first child would take one look at the boxes in the bedroom and would close the door. During the day, we didn't go in there until I had a chance to tidy it up. I was weepy all of the time. Everything my child did was endearing. We'd play together for hours on end, chasing butterflies and bumble bees as we went rolling down the grassy hills. The child in my womb was still quiet.

The town that we lived in was quaint; fall foliage was in full array. However, I was losing my happiness. The man upstairs called one day and was unclear about what he wanted. They had lots of parties up there and you could smell the marijuana. I decided that I had to find a new home. I drove to a town that someone had told me was really nice for young families. I looked up and down the streets. I decided that I would come back again after I found a real estate agent.

Each time that I put my oldest child in the car and drove the hour to this town, I worried that I was tiring out my pregnant self with the stress of finding a new home. I was figuring finances to meet our increasing family needs. Richard came with me on the weekend. We finally found a small home with towering pines in the back yard. We could not see the tops of the trees from the kitchen window. In a month we were loading up a moving trailer and starting another new life. Friends we knew in the area were thrilled.

Up to this point in my life, I was highly functional. I had disciplined myself academically, in work habits and raising a family. My early childhood experiences were of an internal nature and I had learned to withstand intense anxiety in order to accomplish what I wanted to accomplish in many arenas of life.

I had achieved through my hobbies, dance and sailing. A college degree afforded me the chance to teach elementary school as well as college and adult level courses. I became the director of a reading service. I developed many different kinds of relationships. I finessed several types of moves with my husband and children. I was pregnant with my second child as we moved into our first single home. I was a part-time director of a reading service, teaching an extracurricular course for students at a local university.

I was emotional at times with anxiety and eventually depression. I didn't know that the age of twenty- six is known as the average time for bipolar breakdowns in bipolar patients. My thinking was slowly becoming less rational and my moods more unstable. As I like to say, I was not making complete sentences.

CHAPTER SIX

Another Move and Breakdowns
(1974-1980)

Richard and I had our usual fun decorating the new home. We actually had a wood- burning fireplace, a small dining room that looked into the base of tall pine trees, and a bright kitchen with yellow scotch plaid wallpaper. Off the kitchen was a porch that allowed us to enjoy the smells of the piney woods. The house looked compact from the outside but was enough for all our needs. Our second child was born while we lived in our new home. We were as excited and fascinated by this child as the first.

My days were happily spent taking care of the children. After a few years of Richard working in industrial positions, the Nixon trials were on television almost constantly. I told Richard how much the attorneys' demeanor and self-command reminded me of him. The study of law would fit him and coincide with his work in industry.

My mother-in-law was visiting when the mailman brought Richard's acceptance letter to law school. Opening it, I screamed all the way up the back stairs and into the kitchen. She told us years later that I had scared her half to death. I could barely hold my emotions inside anymore. I didn't have a clear-cut action plan for losing my emotions. Richard started law school at night while working a full time personnel position in a paper plant by day.

Polarized

On Monday nights, once a month, the neighborhood arts and crafts club met in a member's home. Coffee was the fare in the afternoons. For a brief time in my existence, I had a sense of belonging to my little family and new friends.

After awhile, however, the daily routine of taking care of the family with Richard gone so much became tedious and boring. The reality of four more years of law school on top of his daily work schedule had an endless quality to it. I would iron his eighteen shirts for work as I always did, watching soap operas and smoking cigarettes. Then I saw something about a charismatic prayer group down at our Catholic church. The church bulletin ad promised an increase in wisdom, knowledge, and understanding of the Holy Spirit. Going to the prayer meetings could enhance your life – at least according to the article.

The Catholic charismatic renewal is a movement within the Catholic church. Worship includes masses and prayer meetings. The belief is that today members of the Christian community have charisms (gifts from the Holy Spirit such as healing, teaching, prophesy), just as the early church members following Jesus' message had in their day (Cor.12, 1,7-10). After Vatican II the movement was a renewal of the people of God. Many people have derived great comfort from participating more fully in the life of the church.

Like all movements, and this is a global movement, there are pitfalls. Some people become overly concerned about the devil. There is no doubt that Satan gets blamed for bad health, bad thoughts, and bad behavior. Little to no reference is made to physical, psychological, and relational factors in the situation. An unhealthy demonic counterpart of super-naturalism developed. This sometimes happens and it is a major obstacle to moral and spiritual maturity when it does. Group pressure to conform in the charismatic renewal can be tyrannical at best, superceding the group's dedication to God. I fell under the group pressure of certain members trying to prove their spiritual powers as healers.

I ventured forth one evening to a charismatic meeting in the basement of the church. The Mass, replete with singing was very emotional. The participants had their hands raised in the air praising the Lord. People moved around kissing and hugging each other. Many of the participants were crying. I was feeling emotional, as our several moves had left me somewhat lonesome, anxious, and isolated. I wondered if this type of gathering was what I was missing in life. I had so much going for myself, yet I thought I needed deeper meaning to complete all that I already had. I sorely needed community to belong to after my travels. The love of Jesus and healing might help.

I was not able to return to a charismatic prayer meeting for several weeks. In the meantime, Richard and I read in the church bulletin about a movement called Marriage Encounter. We had married five years ago almost to the month of August. We agreed that it might be good for us because Richard had such little time. We applied and were accepted. Reverend Bob, a parish priest, asked us for a ride to the weekend that we planned on going. The drive to the other side of the state with Reverend Bob was pleasant. He rode in the back seat as we laughed and joked. We had high hopes for a great weekend that would include learning about new ways to love.

The kickoff for the weekend went well. A team member addressing the sizeable crowd explained that while once you had a wedding ceremony, this weekend you will truly be married. Then two different couples began their presentations on 10-10 dialogues, written conversations between a husband and a wife. They were to be composed of only emotions such as:

"When you kiss me, my face feels warm and pink."

"I feel angry when you forget my birthday. My anger feels flushed with heat in the middle of my chest."

One spouse was to go to their bedroom and the other to remain downstairs in the presenting room. Both were to write for ten minutes, meet in the bedroom and lovingly exchange notebooks to read and respond for another ten minutes. After three or four of these dialogues, Richard and I agreed that our communication system was already decent. So we decided to relax and skip the next session. Uh-oh! That was the wrong choice. Three people came up to our room banging on the door.

"Is your couple love in trouble?" a woman asked, hands cupped against the door.

"All two hundred people are waiting for you downstairs. Open up, please." We were getting dressed as fast as we could.

"This is outrageous," Richard kept muttering.

Outside our bedroom door, the team of volunteers explained. Anytime over the weekend that we didn't show up for a session, it was assumed that we might be in couple trouble. We became more compliant. At Saturday's dinner a cake was in the middle of our dinner table for our fifth anniversary. We didn't have family around to celebrate our special day, so the gesture brought tears to my eyes. Everyone sang, *Happy Anniversary*.

When we ran into Reverend Bob, he was not too happy. His assigned weekend partner was another priest whom he didn't know. They became tired of dialoguing, so they took a walk around the hotel and reported hearing strange noises. They laughed away their loneliness when they realized it was couple love in action.

"How is your weekend going?" Reverend Bob asked with an anguished voice.

"Okay," Richard said.

"Would you think about leaving early?" Reverend Bob asked.

"No, we feel obliged to stay because of the people who made our weekend possible," Richard said as if by apology.

We were the youngest couple on the weekend. Our response was mild compared to couples whose communication system was broken after forty years of marriage and raising families. We listened to the crying and witnessed the embraces of older couples. It was moving and a reminder to the both of us to keep our own dialogues going on a regular basis.

We breathed sighs of relief as we climbed into the front seat of our car. Reverend Bob sat in the back with a roll of toilet tissue to wipe his tears.

His partner, a priest from another state, did not want to continue to stay in touch with him or participate in the 10-10 dialogues. His hopes were dashed for finding a new friend. Richard and I were in an emotional state after such a sensitive weekend.

"Richard and I will dialogue with you," we said. We had observed the leading couples dialoguing with a priest on the weekend team.

"We're glad the weekend is over; it was a little stressful," I reassured him.

"It isn't over. You guys brought a priest here. The Marriage Encounter community has prepared something called an afterglow from the weekend. It is usually small, but because of me it will be a real blowout," he warned us.

The hour and a half ride home gave me time, as tired as I was, to get my thinking really wound up and manic. My manic could be fueled by hurt and covered by exhilaration. I had known hurt in the church and little about being in the limelight. I was wondering how to act with such attention. I glanced over at Richard in the coming dusk. He gave an appearance of not caring one way or another. Perhaps he was dropping the blue cloud and pink flower approach to expressing his emotions.

We arrived at the afterglow, hosted by friends of Reverend Bob, Ed and Harriett. Cars were parked as far as I could see on either side of the street. The home was a split-level, and I screamed all of the way up the stairs into the main section of the home. Richard told me that I was out of control. I had never acted this way before. It turned out to be a symptom in the very beginnings of manic-depressive illness. The environment of the weekend and the afterglow were too emotional for me. I also saw the loving couple that had taken care of our children, and I wanted them to know that their efforts were worth it. I just didn't expect my emotions to take off as they did. Perhaps sitting in the car for the long ride had caused them to bottle up. Jan was there from the charismatic prayer movement. She let me know that I had scared her, too.

Richard and I were hugged, pinched, and kissed in groups of two to four couples. We were handed ample supplies of hors d'oeurves and glasses of wine between hugs. We discussed the favorite parts of the weekend. A fascinating question at the afterglow came from a woman who had no problem showing her coupleness agenda.

"Is Richard going to give up law school to get deeply involved in couple love with you? You could push away the world for couple love," she finished.

We had children to raise and put through college. It might take a good education like Richard was obtaining in law school. However, couple love promising wood-burning fireplaces, wine and cheese, and hugging did sound like a tempting alternative.

The couples were calling, Reverend Bob, our priest, which was far from the truth. Father dug himself out from the piles of admirers and beckoned for us to leave. Hugging and kissing took a long time to get down to the front door and end our Marriage Encounter weekend.

A few weeks later, our priest came to our home armed with his notebook to dialogue. With each passing 10-10 dialogue, he unraveled the story of how he came to live and work in our parish. He was removed from his diocese in the south because of accusations that he had had sex with all the members of a family: husband, wife, and children, that he considered to be his friends. Our diocese had psychiatrists located at a center in our parish boundaries that could help priests so accused. He said he was innocent but suffered from the whole situation. I accepted him and what he had to say.

"You are the most empathic individual I've ever met, Trisha," he said with his voice shaking.

With the information that he was sharing with us, Richard and I became alarmed. Women were inviting me for coffee and quoting scripture about being aware of certain people. They were evasive, but I had a good idea who they might be talking about. There was a mounting negative buzz around church about any of his behaviors. The last wrinkle to all the hidden comments came from Marriage Encounter couples. They no longer called him our priest. Suddenly we were regarded as too young for the 10-10 dialogues with him.

I knew myself to be empathic. However, at that time in my life, Richard was often coming home very late, plus I worried about the children. When Reverend Bob came to dinner for the last time, he asked me if he could read my oldest a bedtime story. I leaned against the wall next to the bed as he read. Without any evidence of wrongdoing, I sadly decided at that moment to end the relationship.

Other problems were on the horizon as well. I went back to the charismatic prayer group meetings and my emotions were starting to match the high swells of feelings during the service. An acquaintance, Jane, who thought that I was still friendly with our priest, suggested that I speak with Sr. Mary Grace at the main charismatic center. It was an old mansion that a religious order had turned into a monastery for the charismatic movement.

"Sr. Mary Grace has a pipeline to God," said Barbara.

"Okay, if I can help Father, I'll go," I said with a sense of relief that I was not to be burdened thinking about his problems. Of course, someone in the religious life could help him more.

It never occurred to Richard or me to inquire about this priest's mental health with any church official. Authority is respected in the Catholic church, and the hierarchy of priests, bishops, cardinals, and the Pope did not like to be questioned. Whatever they were doing for him was becoming suspect, but, to the best of my knowledge, parishioners were not inquiring about him to the church leaders. I thought it was a significant alternative to speak to a nun as they had authority in the church that I did not have.

Authority played a significant part in my own emotional history. The grandiose need to do the impossible regarding this priest was also an impediment to my more rational thinking. To counteract this tendency, I called and made an appointment with Sr. Mary Grace, the nun who everyone in the charismatic prayer group said was incredible to speak with on important spiritual matters.

Polarized

From the moment sister opened the heavy front doors to the monastery, I was uncomfortable. She was a large, overweight woman with a masculine look to her. She took me into a pleasant room with many windows looking out onto the spectacular grounds surrounding the monastery. She didn't seat herself, but kept pulling her slacks up between her legs and shifting her weight from side to side. She spoke in rigid little sayings.

"Praise the Lord," was her response to everything that I said about the church. My bipolar 1 disorder was progressing and interfering with my normal thought processes. At another time, I would have had a pleasant conversation about the rosary and said I'd come back another time for further spiritual discussions. My perceptions were already clouded by my mood swings.

"Sister, I came to speak to you about a priest in my parish," I said.

"I already know whom you mean," she said with intense authority.

"One of my healing teams will be down in your parish's charismatic prayer meeting this spring. We will take care of him," she said with emotional authority.

My head was aching, my anxiety level was increasing and climbing faster and faster up my arms and legs, but I wanted to believe in church authority. My eyesight was making everything in the room seem narrow. Then came the zinger.

"Trisha, evil can attack anyone of us. I believe evil is lurking in your life," she said straight-out.

"The devil has gotten inside of you and is having a picnic," she continued. Although I didn't understand that my manic depression was progressing, I did have the ability to note that she had just met me five minutes ago. She hardly knew my name or anything about me to backup her severe judgments. There must be other reasons.

"You must come to the Lord our God. You must give up any relationship that you can think of with evil forces," she said.

"I know there are evil forces in the world, sister," I said in order to have something to agree with her preaching.

"There are more than you'll ever know. We have discernment at our prayer meetings because it is hard to tell who comes to our prayer meetings with evil intent," she continued to preach.

I had no answer for her. The room was now starting to swim and the bright lights of anxiety were interfering with my mind's ability to concentrate. I did not see any Northern Lights in my mind nor did I think I had any ability to take care of myself. My old images of boundaries that helped me with my limits were erased by this nun's perception that I was evil. I had come to help a priest. At the time I did not understand several factors that were operating. People who profess vows for religious life would help other religious people in trouble before a layperson. I was stepping over my bounds in her eyes. Plus she was new in the community and proving herself as a healer. She wanted the job of healing a priest to add to her credibility in the community.

"I'll handle that priest," she said staking her territory again. As soon as I could, I asked to go home to my family. Suddenly her speech and demeanor toward me changed as we discussed being a wife and mother. That was good. I was back in line with her agendas. I was not happy with the advice my hometown charismatic community leader had given me to see this nun. Once home, I spoke to a friend or two in the group who were shook up that the leadership would send me to her.

I thanked her for her time and ran to my car that was parked in their circular drive. An integrated functioning mind might have laughed her off as a kook. However, she touched many of my old Catholic wounds and beliefs that I was no good. Being close to her God meant I could have no self-confidence in my own way of seeing life.

I stayed home the next few days licking my wounds; or moreover, I was staring into the past reinforcing my badness. At the same time the ambivalent feelings that I was sick and useless didn't add up to 100% of the truth. Eventually the phone rang and it was Reverend Bob. He heard I had gone to visit Sister Mary Grace. I felt guilt as I had gone to elicit help from a nun professed to be a healer and discussed him. I wound up needing help myself. I worried that she had broken my confidence. Then reverend Bob called to say,

"Sister has problems of her own, Trisha," he said in a caring tone that I could barely stand. Guilt followed by frozen tension finally found a slit to accept the sound of his voice.

"The charismatic monastery accepted each religious person on their own merit and ability to contribute to the Lord through the new center that they were building in the monastery. If you threatened her position, you would be rebuffed," he explained.

I appreciated his perspective. She had jabbed at my own self-worth because I might have usurped her role as a healer in the community. This compassionate priest on the phone made me cry. I had felt arid and fearful for so long. I had a little glimpse now as to her motivation in regard to becoming of the charismatic monastery. I had heard that this nun had appeared as very masculine at one time. People were amazed at her continual physical transformation toward the physical appearance of a woman. Charismatic members of my parish meeting took her healthy growth for a charism as a healer, although I did not experience it.

"Did you talk about me?" inquired reverend Bob.

"Yes," I stated with fear. I didn't reveal anything that was discussed. He didn't ask any further questions. I remained in fear that she would actually bring a healing team to save him.

I had walked through a scary story with the charismatic community. I began to look for other friends in the community. I could go to the Newcomers' Club and join an activity that allowed me to get together with other moms and our children. I did join such a group and found some sense of being normal. However, my deteriorating physical illness didn't go along with my efforts at healthy behavior.

I had found too much time to smoke cigarettes and concentrate on Sister Mary Grace's assessment that I was bad at the core of my being. I could not rise above her religious authority. The windstorm of mood swings was rising and crashing inside of me. The power of the chemistry that creates emotions scraped away all rational belief that I was okay, a good Christian, or that God loved me. With each passing scrape the mood swings gained more domination over my mind. Anyone could tell that I was off-center. Healthy minds would laugh off Sr. Mary Graces's own fears and indiscretions.

I pleaded with God to release me from my hateful torments. The children would awake from their naps and I was inspired by their tiny faces to try once again. I wanted to be accepted by one of the deep, meaningful groups I belonged to, not just the lighter and happier groups of women that I was finding.

With Richard only home one night a week, I lived for the phone calls that were still coming from the charismatic renewal group and the Marriage Encounter couples. They were my contact with the outside world. One person called saying she understood that we could not make it to the Marriage Encounter gatherings because of Richard's schedule. Would I consider writing some poetry for the Marriage Encounter Bulletin? I was delighted. I wrote the following poem.

"Romance, Disillusionment, and Joy"
ROMANCE
Your chestnut eyes seemed larger that evening,
Your black hair richer and curlier than usual,
Illusions created by candlelight,
Friendship and wine.

As we listened
Our eyes met with smiles.
So much forgotten
During an afternoon quarrel.

Sharing continued,
The welcoming of a new couple,
Into our circle of friends.

Mellow yellow glow of candles
Reflecting in your eyes.
Your eyes held a kiss
Mine, excited anticipation.

For a split second
I doubted my timing.
Was this kiss now?
Or reflections of the first...

My hand on your knee,
A room humming with happiness
And warmth.
A room warmer for our love!

DISILLUSIONMENT

I saw anxiety pace across your face
In the early breakfast conversation
It's always nothing, nothing,
Nothing shared under the table,
Nothing forced down with gulps of tea.

My quest for dialogue
Met with a furrowed brow,
Love letters buried again
Under a pile of legal briefs.

If caring equals sharing,
I find it a bitter pill to swallow,

For where is the caring,
If there are no written words to share?

We alone share the crosses
We bear.
I've no power to pluck fear from
Your eyes.
Share it with me for a while.

Merely easing the pain,
Merely easing the fog.
Hurry, love,
I grow impatient…

JOY

Beethoven's 9th was filling the church
On a brilliant August morn.
We supported each other with
Interlaced arms,
Leaving the altar in a state of joy,
Innocently imagining a life of
Continual bliss.

O come, come sing a song of joy,
For we shall love each other!

Is this word called joy a singular feeling?
Or an encompassing state of being?
Years have passed,
Wisdom has mellowed our lives,
I thought I loved you that August morn,
But days unfold with signs of love.

Polarized

Oh come, come sing our song of joy,
For we do love each other!

Two years ago we shared a weekend,
A weekend that never seems to end.
Each new surge of joy
Leaves me hungry for the next.
And waits each year under our
Christmas tree.

O come, come sing our song of joy,
For we still Love each other!

Each phase partakes of the whole,
Romance, Disillusionment, or Joy,
All come full circle,
In the beginning, middle, or end.
Can many books explain it?
What does it matter?

Who cares what's fair?
The foolish and the wise?
Is it only one word?
Oh yes, my Love, yes.

So come, come sing our song of joy,
For we love each other!

Trisha Frisch (1975)

I was proud of the poem, and Richard loved it, too. The Marriage Encounter community printed the poem, but my copy of the bulletin did not show up in the mail. Thinking it was an oversight, I went to the woman's house where the bulletin was edited. She told me that they didn't have any left. She instructed me to go to another couple I knew, Harry and Alison. When I arrived at their home, they told me all of the good things they were doing through Marriage Encounter. They had necklaces in French that said I love you more today than yesterday. Also, they had just had a party for Marriage Encounter couples from France. They had really enjoyed couple love in French.

"You ought to get your own," she said as she finally handed me her copy of the bulletin to take home. I looked at her knowing she meant a marriage, not a bulletin. Off and on, comments were still made regarding my husband's decision for law school. All of the people commenting had made the decision for couple love and spending a lot of time together. Our way of being a couple was obviously distained.

I continued to spend a great deal of time on the phone while the children were napping. I wanted my mom and Richard's parents to come and visit. They did come, but then I was alone again as a single mom with Richard in school. No one thought to ask me over from the groups where life happened in the right way. We did have other friends but law school limited the time we had to socialize as a couple. Marriage Encounter was regarded as a movement that wasn't for everyone. I never critized the movement to others as it did have many good points, including improving communication skills.

My friends in the city were working, and I saw some of them from time to time. I had grown overly sensitive to people I would meet downtown when I was shopping. I had felt periods of rejection before in junior high and high school, but this time the feelings were going to be compounded with other problems.

As always Richard and I built a very warm and welcoming environment in our home. I was lifted up by the smell of the pines and the sun slanting through those mighty pine trees. Some days I felt one with the spiritual experience that nature can evoke. Sometimes my arms and face felt as if air was inside, and I was being lifted up. I only told my friends that I had a physical sense of oneness with nature, as I didn't want to appear out of the ordinary. The times I was in the woods were so exquisite. I could sense that Richard felt badly about how things had turned out for me with Marriage Encounter. He was at work and school all day. He suggested that we present to the Marriage Encounter community in someone's home. It was supposed to be a talk about what our marriage looked like, a picture of us. The lecture was called, *An Image*.

Okay. Maybe if they heard us together we'd find some friends in the Marriage Encounter community that we could relate to. We wrote our scripts for weeks beforehand. We spoke at the home of the people who had originally babysat for us on our first weekend. They were very hospitable as always. We were very clear about our dedication to each other and each other's careers.

"Law school is very dry," Richard said that evening while smiling to the group. We left realizing that we were really in the wrong group, a minority of one professional couple. Most of the people were ten to twenty years older, and people who worried about our couple love. If we had lived in the city, I might have found more friends. Richard and I grew up in suburbia and believed that we would be the most comfortable there. Moving because of the army, company changes, and law school had left me void of friends, especially staying home for our family life.

I found some woman friends at a party one night across town. The group became a major source of friendship. They dabbled in the New Age. I reiterated over and over that I was a Catholic and not interested in their beliefs. Strangely, they accepted my beliefs and never pushed themselves on me. It was so refreshing after all of the other groups. I watched them get involved in witchcraft, without ever expecting me to join. I didn't want to when I saw the personal demise of such activities. When one friend left a covenant, she took the time to warn me about how destructive that lifestyle really was. We talked a lot and she eventually became a Christian on her own inclinations. I felt wonderful about that experience. It remains a positive memory. Mostly, their behavior was quite Christian.

In all of the days I experienced loneliness, something odd was starting to happen. One day on my way to work, I went along a road that was sheltered by a tunnel of leaves. Tiny thoughts of being evil kept popping into my mind. I didn't have any control over when the obsessive thoughts started or ended. They were like pinpricks. I'd go to work and forgot about it. Off and on in the next few weeks, the same obsessive-compulsive event would happen. The frequency and duration increased. Within six weeks, these tiny uncontrollable one or two word thoughts were constant, coupled by a debilitating exhaustion. I noticed one thing that was in the plus column. The mood swings that were of tornado size were not happening. These thoughts were almost dry and my emotions were manageable even though the thoughts were enormously painful.

In search for companionship, I called an old friend to come and visit us. Sarah was a social worker. She was very earthy as well as sophisticated in her ways of dealing with life. She asked if she could bring along her housemate, a man named Brian. We were happy to see them. After a few visits, Brian asked Richard if he would hire a few of his friends to work in Richard's plant. Richard said that he could do that for him as a friend.

I took a frantic call from my husband during this early stage of obsessive-compulsive disorder. The plant where he worked had received bomb threats, and he let the people go home. Hundreds of workers screamed in five different languages as they ran out of the plant. It was enormously frightening for all of the staff, too.

The staff discovered that Brian and his friends belonged to the October league. It was founded in 1971 and had grown out of the radical student organization, Students for a Democratic Society. It was the predecessor organization to the Communist Party (Marxist-Leninist) that was a Maoist political party in the U.S.A. (Wikipedia.org/wiki/Communist_Party_(Markist-Leninist)(USA)

Brian and his friends were identified as being involved in the bomb threat. Richard was extremely concerned about the children's safety and mine. He wanted me to know that police and bomb experts were watching our home. I was terrified. I called my old friend from the charismatic prayer group, Jan, and asked if she could take the kids and me in for the night. I told her what happened.

"Praise the Lord! Come right over," Jan said. I felt relieved.

I tried to sleep in her home and couldn't.

"Stare at my crucifix and you will fall asleep," Jan comforted me. It didn't work.

"I'm going to call the monastery to prepare a room for you. The way you feel, the Lord's place will be the safest for you," said Jan.

"You can leave the kids with me," she generously offered.

The charismatic monastery was the last place in the whole wide world that I wanted to go. However, I had no money for a motel room and I surely was not going home. So I left hoping that Richard would eventually find my note in the kitchen at home. It described the whereabouts of his little frightened family.

At the monastery, I was greeted by Sister Mary Grace and taken up to the main chapel. Reverend Greg, one of the chaplains, was standing behind some kneeling retreatents. He explained that they were praying in tongues, a form of prayer from Corinthians in the Christian scriptures. I exclaimed that I prayed in the same language. He explained in his own terms that the residents who worked in the monastery had to be careful about the people who stayed there. He said,

"Your prayers were probably from evil." I could not earn their trust as the first impression had had a strong influence on them.

"I have seen folks go on and on with your kind of problems. You can try psychologist and psychiatrists, but your chances are poor for a good

Christian life," said Reverend Greg. I thought that I had been condemned to hell fire on earth. I was allowed to spend the night. I spent most of my time reading the bible that Reverend Greg gave me. It was as if I was slowly being converted to their brand of Christianity. Sister Mary Grace took me up many steps to a cement bedroom. She told me that right below me, if I should need anything, was a couple who slept with votive candles on an altar all night.

I hardly slept and mostly wondered when my anxiety, lodged in my arms and legs, would go away. Once I went down the steps that had no railing and talked to the coupled whose room was ablaze with candles. They were annoyed and told me to go back to sleep. At 5:00 in the morning I went for a walk outside with a mind fixated on scripture. I would know resurrection if I only begged forgiveness for my evil and praised the Lord. I went inside to get something to eat and call Richard. I had to wait a minute while the phones were unlocked. Sister Mary Grace explained that phone use distracted from prayer. I found Richard at home and he came to pick me up as well as the kids from Jan's. I was praying with scripture in the car ride to Jan's house.

"Will you put that thing away?" Richard yelled at me with both fear and anger. I placed it in my bag in the back seat. When we were all reunited, Richard cooked us dinner and I finally fell fast asleep.

One night when Richard was in law school, I found a babysitter and went to the monastery. They were having a prayer meeting and the nave of the chapel looked especially beautiful with lights shining on the wooden arch above the altar. Mary, one of the leaders from the group spotted me as I came into the chapel.

"What brings you here?" said Mary with pointed curiosity.

"I want to be prayed over for a complete healing," I said with exhaustion. My obsessions and emotions were dragging me beyond my usual level of hope that this pain would ever end.

Several people came over to pray over me. Sister Mary Grace joined the group and prayed that I'd receive a sign of joy. She even wrote it on a chalkboard. I watched the faces of the men and women. A stable place inside of me reassessed the whole situation. I felt good from this place inside. I believed in myself for just a little while and jumped up from my chair. I threw my arms up in the air and told the group I was feeling joy. They all smiled and praised the Lord. I moved toward the door and left, never to return.

When I reached home, I still had with some self-confidence left. I got out my key to open the front door. It gave in a little too easily as Richard was on the other side, not the babysitter.

"Make an appointment with the mental health clinic in the morning," he said firmly. I went to a local mental health clinic and was tested. I was frightened and when they asked me to draw pictures, I remember drawing life as a huge monster. It overwhelmed the pictures of a man and a woman that I drew. It's just that we didn't have any money to pay the price of the clinic's therapy. Toward the end of the month, we often ate peanut butter and jelly on heels of bread. We didn't want to lose our house. We had the children to worry about. Relatives said we would regret it if Richard left law school. So I didn't go back to the clinic.

Thank God for cigarettes. They held me together as I was alone with two children and I became more and more isolated. I called my childhood psychologist friend, Norman Berk, and he referred me to a doctor near our home that he had heard might help in cases of religious problems. He was a Cognitive-Behavioral Therapist (CBT) psychologist and only charged $25.00 per hour.

The psychologist met me at a Catholic college in a classroom building. I learned relaxation exercises. He wanted me to take them slowly and really memorize what I was doing. He told me to do something for myself. I had no money but I started to buy two candy bars on the way to see him. I'm sure that was not what he meant, but it was what I could afford. The depression meant I wasn't eating much anyway. He talked a great deal about behavior modification. He did not discuss medication.

The next week I learned more about the relaxing exercises and we practiced them. The third week was the final lesson on relaxing exercises. He also introduced thought stopping. It was similar to a mantra. I tried really hard to stop the thoughts. I remember walking around the mall one day as I shopped and said stop. In the long run, I said stop for twenty hours with no luck. He taught me to act as if nothing was bothering me. For example, at a party I was to try and smile a lot more than usual. That skill, Acting As If, worked really well except I was not around other people often enough to use the skill.

He explained that I was building negative thought chains if I didn't stop the first thought. I really wanted to build positive thought chains, one positive thought after another. If any of my positive thoughts were broken into by a negative thought, I was to take a breath, thought stop, and say the positive thought again.

We talked about the situations, individuals, and groups in my life that may have led up to my Obsessive-Compulsive Disorder (OCD). No medical or physical reasons were accounted for at this point. Some of my past experiences with religion had added up in a quirky way. Religious authority figures telling me that I had come from evil fed into my underlying religious fears of the past. The specific connections were still somewhat vague. Exhausted, my mind protected itself from further harm and disintegration with OCD. Medication was a necessary aide that this psychologist refused to consider.

We continued with the skills. Self-talk, which is talking to myself with positive and/ or directive messages, might help me before the thought stopping. My self-talk was interrupted by OCD. We tried relaxation methods and picturing troublesome scenes until the fear of the scenes were gone. It is called guided imagery. When the psychologist was at his wits end, he announced that he was going on vacation. He wanted me to go to a center and see a therapist who would delve into my sexual problems. I knew I didn't have any of those problems, so I waited for him to return from vacation and made an appointment.

"We'll try some more," he said.

Polarized

I saw him for almost a year before the OCD stopped pulsing through my brain. I felt so relieved and happy. I thought I was a candidate for sainthood that year. We talked a lot about my frightening background with religion. We didn't spend any time talking about a whole parish/community that was disturbed by a bishop's decision to send the pathological priest miles away from his diocese. Today we see these illegal situations mentioned over and over again in places such as the Sexual Abuse Tracker, 2001.

Now I had friends, a cousin I saw from time to time, and I was skinny from the depression that I had just survived. Richard was getting closer to our goal of finishing law school. I also worked as a hostess in a New England restaurant. When I first took the job, I could not read the menu. The internal imbalances were still making all of the letters wavy when I looked at a page of print. I forced myself to read as I had lost my ability to read. I accomplished what seemed be a great achievement. I joined the League of Women Voters, found friends, and intellectual stimulation that helped me to read again, too.

My waitress outfit was a badge of honor for me in the tavern. I could now read the menus, take orders, and run around the downstairs tavern listening to the piano. I had a world that was just mine for a few hours, four times a week. The people at the bar were usually outrageous. The bar tender was an amusing man to talk to once in awhile. The other waitresses would come and go with various life stories to tell in the prep room. I liked the food and everyone smoked cigarettes, so I felt a sense of belonging. Throughout my life, belonging was like a light switch that went on or off. I loved it when it was on.

Richard stopped by on his way home from school for a drink. Sometimes I paid for it out of my tip money. Richard enjoyed our unique way of seeing each other while the bartender thought he was mooching. With the fun, my problems were far behind.

Richard was getting upset at the way I was house keeping. When he said anything, I would stand back even further from my cleaning responsibilities. One afternoon, I became aware that the house was in shambles. I had made a mess on purpose. I began to establish my authority in the household one step at a time. When I was finished with my ideas, Richard liked it but he wouldn't stay out of my territory. He had his own problems. When he was anxious he would immediately try to control.

I had a few good months. Then in January or February, I was invited to go to a women's day at a women's college. The main speaker was talking about Genesis and the time of the sharing that was coming soon. Photographers from the local Catholic newspaper and the city paper were in the front row. Someone said that the reporters from the Catholic newspaper were not a friendly group.

Women's position in the Catholic church has always had strict limits and boundaries designed by the male hierarchy. The nuns and lay women presenting at the conference were women who wanted to set their own agenda in the church and break those limits and boundaries as being unfair. There were seminars to attend lead by women ministers. I went to one by a woman who owned and operated a homeless shelter for women. She wore a roadster cap. She so impressed me that I went out and bought a cap like hers.

My religious instability sent me into manic laughing. The friend, Tori, who I had come with to the lecture, took me into the bathroom. I finished my manic laughing in there and returned to finish hearing the new ideas of the day. The material conflicted with a lifetime of guilt and underlying lack of valuing myself as a woman. That day, coupled with the bipolar disorder, was about to send me into a hospital.

CHAPTER SEVEN
Hospitalizations (1976-1980)

After the women's conference in the city, my desire to help others became overwhelming. I became overwrought at the thought of my plight in the Catholic church as a woman. In retrospect, once again my severe lack of development of a strong self-concept with self-confidence was alarming. This time my grandiosity led me to believe that it was time to resolve the war between the sexes. Equality must be on its way when it came to decisions and positions in the hierarchy of the church. The only thing that I accomplished was to destroy my stability with a manic swing. I became so overwrought about changing the world problems that I gave up sleeping.

Three nights of absolutely no sleep with strong anxiety coming up and down my arms sent me to morning Mass. The other women at church surrounded me, saying I looked exhausted, and that I was not making sense. One offered to take care of my baby for the day. A young priest asked me into the rectory to relax and talk.

I talked all day. Around 4 in the afternoon, I asked them to call Richard at work. Before he came, I remember being so weak that I was lying down on the floor. I was talking about inviting the whole world to a party, including the Eskimos. I think my psychotic babbling grew out of my loneliness as well as bipolar disorder.

"That's a lot of people, Trisha," he gently commented. He just kept listening and responding. Why he never called for medical help or my husband, I'll never know.

Richard finally came to literally carry me home. My friend returned my baby a few hours later. I remember her gently holding my hand on the edge of the bed.

"How come such a lovely lady was paying attention to me now?" I asked.

"I owe you one," she said with a smile.

Richard called other friends who did not understand my plight and were giving Richard their own agendas as to why they couldn't come to take the children. He needed some help and at that point I didn't know why he needed it.

I was supposed to try to sleep. I felt like an angel with gossamer wings trying desperately to fly off the bed. An angry God, all red and fiery appeared on the ceiling.

Richard decided to call my psychologist. He told me to drink hot toddies, more than one if I had to in order to go to sleep. Four hot toddies later I was still in anguish and exhaustion.

In the morning, naked, I walked into the other room where piles of unfolded laundry now existed to find some clothes. As I turned around, I saw my mother-in-law. Richard had picked her up at the airport. Not knowing what was going on, I was just relieved that a family member had come to help. Richard had frightened me by saying we could lose our children if someone didn't help. He called my mom but she didn't understand what was wrong with me. Why does she have to go to the hospital? Mom had her job to consider and couldn't come to help. Richard took me to the emergency room.

On the half hour ride to the hospital, I prayed with my bible. When we pulled into the emergency room parking lot, I still did not understand that I might be hospitalized. We walked into the waiting area and up to the desk. I was smiling and cooperative for the first two minutes. Then a form was placed in front of me. I filled it out haphazardly. The intake person pointed out mistakes that I had to correct. I became belligerent about filling in the information. I said that there was no reason to fill in my middle name. What was this all about? I wasn't staying. Richard came behind me and enfolded me in his arms.

I was escorted into a room and asked to sit on a bed. Richard was right by my side. Groups of interns and residents kept coming in to look at me. Stare at me was more like it. Then the psychologist who was the director of the psychiatric unit came in. I thought he looked like he was intellectually challenged. I felt some irrational connection; I tried to kiss him. He backed off and told me that such behavior was inappropriate. He left and I started screaming about the devil. I could also see a gurney being rolled into my view out in the hallway. Someone told me I had to sign the admission form or be taken to a locked unit.

I looked at the admissions form and saw the diagnosis: acute schizophrenic hysteria. I ripped it up, screaming again. The psychologist came to say that they were going to give me one more chance. Richard was by my side. In my exhaustion I talked about many things including his time in law school and that once he wanted to be a doctor.

"If I sign the papers will the hospital make you a doctor, Richard?" I stated in my exhaustion and confusion. In the hallway I could see the gurnie waiting for me to go to a locked unit.

"Yes," he said.

"Will you come upstairs and take care of me if I sign it?" I asked in anguish.

"Yes," he said calmly. I signed it and everyone in the room started to move.

I was picked up by five people to be placed on a bed. I resisted with my high level of manic energy. Being a great dancer, I'd swing in the opposite direction from their every effort to control me. Up and down, side-to-side, we twisted around. They won. I was immediately turned onto my side, shot with thorazine, and the manic beasties were silenced in under a minute. I was speaking like an adult. When I calmed down a nurse brought me a sandwich to eat. I ate a tuna fish sandwich that tasted delicious mostly because I was starving. I asked a lot of questions about the unit upstairs. Richard was still in one piece by my side.

Once I finished my sandwich, Richard walked beside my bed as the nurses took me upstairs. I slid off the bed in the psychiatric unit. I was going to have a single room because of a forty-eight hour observation. The time limit produced tension flooding through my veins for I could still go to a locked unit. The possibility was held over my head for two weeks, causing me to focus on tasks at hand. Also, I smoked lots of cigarettes because it conflicted with the manic feeling of total freedom. The cigarettes became my boundaries.

When I arrived and got settled in my room, I went out to a little sitting area to smoke. Some exhausted people were blowing the smoke in the wrong direction, out and not in. The ashes were falling everywhere. I was there, too. Their behavior made me think that my view of reality was probably not back on target as I thought it was while eating my tuna fish sandwich in the emergency room. I was also very, very exhausted. Other patients sitting in the same area had shoeboxes full of poetry sitting at their feet. One or two patients were writing and a few patients were thumbing through their boxes.

I asked one woman what was in her box?

"Poetry," was her answer; I told her it was amazing. She stated that she was just messing around. I got around to asking the group if they were authors. It certainly looked like a talented group. I got the same answer about messing around. My mind was racing with mania and my thoughts were along the lines of hoping that we could put together a poetry reading or a booklet of many of their poems. When I shared my idea, a spokesman for the group said clearly that they were not at that point right now. They were just messing around.

The structure of the psychiatric unit ascribed to the belief system of Cognitive Behavioral Therapy (CBT). We were expected to keep a strict schedule in order to stay on the unit. The morning meeting discussed daily plans for activities; group therapy intensely covered our need to accept our failures and to begin again. With new thoughts and behaviors we would affect our feelings and change our lifestyle patterns.

Occupational Therapy and individual sessions were places to continue to work on changing our belief systems to rational thinking and behaving. I went over and over the process of relaxing my thinking that led to depression and manic episodes. I never did guided imagery. My imagination was very strong. I did not need to be disturbing my imagination. However, the staff was impressed that I ordered my own diet food tray, true CBT in practice.

I was expected to eat in a small glass enclosed room where the staff could observe me. It was difficult to get the food up to my mouth due to the exhaustion and perhaps the effect of the meds. The thorazine seemed to make me stiff. I dropped food all over me those first few nights. I was also told that I would be on staff watch, and I had to keep my bedroom door ajar. I couldn't sleep no matter what I tried. I would pray and pray and pray. I would convince myself to go to sleep so I didn't have to go to a locked unit.

"S-s-sush," said a male patient who came to my door one evening. I was scared and started to make noises.

"Don't disturb the desk!" he said, as I yelled for the nurse. I was afraid he might hurt me. People were somewhat stable but there was always the chance of violence. He took off and never bothered me again. In the community meetings he acted as if nothing happened. I was hypervigilent from that moment forward.

I spoke to my nurse, Jan the next day because we were encouraged to talk with our assigned staff about anything that happened on the psychiatric floor. We could learn from any situation. She said that violence could happen anywhere out there in society. Most days we are safe, but we all have to take care of ourselves. She continued that there are no assurances of safety in life. The hospital does its best to protect folks, but it is unrealistic to believe anyone has 100% safety in or out of the hospital.

I did sleep about four hours the first nights. One night I was asleep when it was time for my meds. Two nurses had to drag me to the meds station outside. I was informed that the next time I was to get there myself. So, most nights, I didn't bother to try to sleep until after the 2 a.m. meds. If I lay down on the floor to try and sleep, I couldn't get up. I was sore all over. Anxiety was certainly a component.

The patients I met ranged from bizarre to unaware of their own value, to fairly normal, whatever that is in reality. I was afraid because this was my peer group. The fear eventually subsided; I thanked God for my lot in life. I was going to do whatever was necessary to go forward into mental health. I was in the unit for seven weeks. I had plenty of time to observe patient behavior. The healthy thought that I was not going to submit myself to a life of illness crept into my mind more and more often. Jan told me to take advantage of everything on the unit to grow and adapt to life with my illness. I sure did.

I liked starting the day with the community meetings. The leader wore a beret like the woman, Kip, who presented at the Catholic convention. She always started the conversations by asking what were folks going to do that day? It was a really challenging question for a group like us.

Some people were going to have visitors. Others were allowed to go home for the day. Each of us had a schedule. We would talk about what we were making in occupational therapy or what we planned on eating for lunch that was nutritious. Everyone had two individual counseling sessions a day, and some of us had group therapy. I didn't have group therapy during the first hospitalization because my thought process was not strong enough.

Writing group was my most difficult therapeutic session because emotions were incorporated. Bipolar 1 disorder means that strong mood swings take over the thought process as well as the proper functioning of the emotions. Until the medication takes effect, trying to express emotions is very painful. The mental health leaders in charge of the group would give us topics that would naturally stabilize emotions and thoughts. Just as physical therapy exercises people's muscles, we had to exercise our thoughts and emotions.

Physical exercise was open to all. We had to be on time for meds. We could play games, the piano, watch TV a little bit, go to the music room, or discuss the nighttime activities we wanted to choose. Scheduling was a must. It had to be reviewed by our individual counselor. The whole staff was pleasant but strict about adhering to our schedule commitments. I finally got to speak with Jan, who gave me individual counseling. I had a lot on my mind from the day. People knew I was fearful in writing group, and they all made faces and yelled at me. So we talked.

Jan's conversations continually guided my perceptions. There was no real safety anywhere, but it was secure on the unit. I had to take care of myself in many ways rather than relying on others to be perfect toward me, treating me with kid gloves. I started to realize that my gifts and talents were the places to put my sensitivity, not hanging on every comment that others made.

One day I realized that any mortal could appear to be approachable or not approachable. Positive energy is holistic and people can instinctively tell when you are not in sync. Naturally, smiling always helps. "Acting As If'" became a significant cognitive behavioral skill. It means something like smiling when you'd rather cry, because you are attempting to fit back into society. It is not pretentious or phony because the goal is to match positive behavior to a situation in the hope that the emotions and behavior will be congruent. Writing my thoughts, irrational and rational, calmed my emotions.

Jan and I talked about everything just like friends. The psychiatrist dropped the thorazine and added major tranquilizers. I had some jealousy because the bipolar people took lithium, and they seemed to do better than I was doing. They left the unit sooner and struck me as highly functional. I was there for seven weeks, and I saw lots of patients leave. It made me feel bad, but it also helped me see my diagnosis: Schizophrenia. Later in life, some doctors laughed about my entrance diagnosis, saying they had thrown the book at me (acute schizophrenic hysteria).

Family was another journey. The patient phone was in use all night long, and they were usually yelling at someone. Jan said that it was the people in the outside world who put the most pressure on the patients. They were the ones that got the brunt of their anger. For instance, I got annoyed at my mother who wouldn't come to help out. She had to work. Still, she didn't seem to understand that I was ill. Buried feelings toward my husband came tumbling out. Where were the flowers? I had stood beside him for four long years of school. His mother was staying with him to help with the kids. He knew that I was safe and getting treatment. So it was difficult to say I wanted some loving attention from him, but I did. The resulting tea roses were beautiful. I put them near my head when I couldn't sleep.

In the midst of these hospital memories, I have to say that a certain frustration, a certain self-hatred was never addressed. So much ground had to be covered in several sessions a day that I never looked at the basis that drove me mad second by second. I had grown up in such an authoritarian environment at home and school that I had learned to bury myself. Short of being emotionally irresponsible in an environment where I was already in trouble, I completely buried the elements of the past that continued in some measure to destroy my happiness in the moment.

I had done what I was told as a good Catholic girl. I had held back my human nature when others saw it as their God given human rights. I overate whenever my emotions swelled, not only to avoid a manic swing or depression, but also to avoid emotions that would throw my world loop-de-loop. I continued to protect myself with food.

I'm articulate. The nurses took turns dialoguing with me as I named it. I had so much inside of me that I was trying to integrate that my pressured speech was very pronounced. They were honest in acknowledging that they did not wish to go over their time limits with me, but I was valuable to their learning process. One of the staff men in writing group declared that despite being gay, he loved me and was sexually attracted to me. He had had some experience with women and had to process his feelings for me before I left. It slowly increased my self-esteem that he needed me, too, even though a patient.

I tried to starve myself emotionally for the future of my family. It was way too much to expect of someone with my emotional nature and education. It was pointed out to me in future hospitalizations that some relatives could not cope with my needs to express myself as a human.

I learned to spend more of my free time in the hospital alone. I avoided the sinking feelings I received from the world around me as to who I was and what my behavior demanded. I was always compromising what I needed for myself. I mused: are not the racing thoughts of the bipolar mind nothing more than the rapid tears of boredom foisted on it by a dull thinking segment of society? Are not my tears a response to the demands of the culture? - one that does not afford a woman the chance to grow beyond the expected? I acquiesced to others' needs, becoming a sad portion and cup.

However, it took three hospitalizations for me to realize that a lot of my inability to care for my developmental needs stemmed from the basic lack of medication to calm my physical illness. I did finally accept medication as a permanent part of my medical compliance the last three hospitalization. It became a significant part of my stability.

"The truth shall set ye free, but first it will make ye miserable," was one-woman patient's unbeatable saying about mental illness in a community meeting. Everyone in the meeting laughed. Experiences with other people began to pull me together. The hospital experiences were becoming empowering.

A few other people came to visit me. Kathleen had taken her turns caring for the children from the beginning. My cousin and my aunt came one day with a plant, a book, and a candle. We sat in the community room and lit a candle. Immediately we were asked to blow it out. I was so happy that they came to visit; I thought the whole room was watching us. Nurse Jan assured me that my observations were off this time. I had merely noticed myself being noticed by my visitors.

The young man who composed music but never had the courage to play in public went to the piano. My guests were amazed at his abilities. After they left, nurse Jan continued to reinforce, in her blunt manner, that I was not the center of attention. The other patients in the gathering room were busy with their own agendas. Grandiosity in a bipolar patient can lead him/her to believe that she/he is the center of attention. We can have exaggerated perceptions of how important we are. While I was enjoying my guests, the other patients were also enjoying their activities in the gathering room. All of the patients were the center of attention as far as staff was concerned.

A social worker, Miss Reddy, came for a visit. I had known her from doing volunteer work across the street in a psychiatric halfway house. Neither Jan nor others on staff particularly welcomed her. Jan asked,

"Did you have an appointment to see Patricia?" Jan asked.

"No," she said.

"I only came to visit," she continued.

"You needed an appointment to see Trisha," Jan replied with annoyance in her voice. The social worker smiled kindly and said good-bye to me.

"Haven't you had enough humility?" said Jan. I gathered Jan's fear was that Miss Reddy would ask me to come over as a client to the place where I had done volunteer work. I didn't understand the full impact of their confrontation. It would take humility to take further treatment in a facility where I had done volunteer work. However, if I needed the care, I thought it was up to me to make that decision.

I was slowly discerning my decision to be content within myself with change; I needed less ideals and more practicality. The hurtful emotion that triggered a manic reaction was related to the pain of not being an enclosed self. My marriage to Richard and our young family was emotionally rattled in several ways before the hospitalization. My interest in helping someone else, a priest who was regarded by disturbed, self-centered religious fanatics as evil. My childhood underpinnings and my physical disorder were not strong enough to blow it off.

During my hospital stay, I was becoming less wired to cultural expectations and more flexible as a human being. When my weight problem kept increasing, I didn't see that the food and wine I drank were the plates and cups of others' visions. It would take years to feel what I knew. My life and marriage had a special seasoning to it that did not include anyone else. I began to recognize more readily others good cheer, as well as jealousy and distortions.

During seven long weeks in the hospital, I missed my husband and children. I masked most of this missing with manic feelings. The hospital psychiatric occupational therapy center became the place where I took care of the hurt, anger, and high anxiety components of my manic swings. I was allowed to participate in various arts and crafts. For example, I would take a piece of aluminum and bang on it, creating a shape I'd like. The first try included banging upon it until it hit the ceiling. The occupational therapist came over and told me to slow down. She slipped it away from me as quickly and as gently as she could. She saved it for days when I looked calmer, promising me that I could bang on it for just a few minutes, as long as I controlled what I was doing.

Another afternoon, I decided to practice my relaxing exercises. I chose a spot behind the TV area where nobody was watching TV and I was tensing and relaxing muscles as I lay on my back. The nurse who drew the strongest boundaries, especially in the writing group, Wilma, came rushing over to tell me I could be alarming other patients. They might think I was having heart failure or something else. They would not understand what I was doing. I must go to my bedroom and practice there at the end of the day. We could not stay in our bedrooms during the day. I always thought that she overreacted to the patients. In writing group I told her and she accepted my feedback. After a while I realized that the staff wanted me to express myself and it always reduced the manic feelings.

I was a fairly reasonable patient. Once a bunch of us got together in the music room and prayed together. This was sort of off limits and it made us feel very good to be doing something behind the staff's back. I imagine some areas like the music room were set up with a dash of privacy to release some of the tension of following a schedule with many limits.

The psychologist in charge of the unit, Dr. Robert told me that I had impressed him. I had an inner ability to observe my own behavior; I remembered the tumultuous entry into the hospital, where he intuitively gave me a second chance to sign the admission paper. (I did not tell him that he looked intellectually disabled to me that day in the emergency room). He looked very professional sitting behind the desk in his office.

Later in the day I was speaking to one of the women on staff. I asked if I could have access to my own records.

"You don't want to read them," she said.

"I want to write a book someday about myself and my psychiatric experiences," was my retort.

"Yes, Trisha," said the counselor with a little disbelief in her voice.

All of the patients who came onto the unit from other hospitals concurred one the same point.

"This unit is the best in the area. It is bright and cheerful. It is known as the penthouse of psychiatric units." These statements were always reassuring to me and the other patients. We were trying hard to get our lives back in order. The care was excellent. The mandatory limits and boundaries worked for me. After a few weeks, Jan asked me to try and do anything I wanted to accomplish. It was so hard to think about what I might like for myself. Slowly, I could one or two things in the same day.

All of the external structure and efforts at internal thought changes began to have an effect on my perceptions of my hospitalizations and my life to come after I left. I did make a visit home toward the end of my first hospitalization, and I remember looking around my home and seeing things that I wanted to clean up or change. Some things just looked irrational: the way I stacked dishes in the closet, or the way I had folded laundry. I just had a better-organized mind from all of the support in the hospital.

The kids were not home when I visited. They were still living with their grandparents. With the exception of phone calls, I had not seen them in five weeks. Feelings of missing them were covered over by my needs to get myself straightened out. I really wanted to so that I could be there for them. My husband was holding up fairly well, missing the family for seven weeks. I was manic when I returned to the hospital.

So I told the nurse on duty that I felt very tense. I remember having worn my yellow Easter dress. Wilma always drew the limits quickly, yet she told me to put on my sneakers and go running around the block outside a few times. I did and it worked. It inspired both exercise and my love of dance to return.

One afternoon right before I left the first time, I noticed some cards on a shelf above the beds in my room. I got up upon a chair, reached for them, and dusted them off. They were get-well cards. On the back, the prices were crossed off, and 5 cents was written in their place. I had come to understand that folks with a psychiatric diagnosis were not full price individuals or patients.

Dr. Kane was my very first psychiatrist. He was nice and his medications were helping me to be able to follow CBT. My outside CBT psychologist was still on my treatment team. He had told me again as soon as I got out of the hospital that he wanted me off the medication. He said that in the long run it would make me sick. Nobody told me that in the hospital. So, not having gotten over my complete trust in the authority of this outside psychologist, I got off the meds. Besides, this might mean that I was returning to be a 50-cent card person, not a 5-cent card person.

I wanted to thank all of my visitors while I was in the hospital, so I saved all of the flowers petals from the arrangements people had sent me. I found pretty light plaid material and made sachets filled with the crushed flower petals. I invited people over for lunch and made soufflés. Everyone really liked my gift. I slowly wound down from the worst of the manic swing. It looked like I was going to live in neutral and be all right.

I continued to see my outside psychologist. However, without medication, I slid into a major depression replete with OCD. I was back in the hospital within six months.

Wilma reassured me several times that the medication had worked for other people and that it would work for me. I was to be patient. The painful, obsessive-compulsive thoughts lifted after awhile and I felt better. I left with plans to stay at home and raise the kids with a few activities for myself. I was thankful to be home for Christmas.

I tried to conduct an exercise program in my home for a small fee. A few neighbors came. The only problem was that trying new behavior started to activate old symptoms. I needed to do what Jan, in the hospital, said to me,

"Don't be afraid to sit back and let others come to you. You are always out there giving." I did not have the discernment for noticing the difference between energy draining activities and energy building activities. Guilt always led me toward events where I had to give more than receive.

The hospital team of the second visit had said I was to stay on medication. Once again my outside psychologist told me to stop the meds. Accepting the medication is one of the largest stumbling blocks to mental health for most folks. The hospital team also recommended that my husband, Richard, take me away to another state. The change of environment would be very good for my health. I would be away from all the reminders of my illnesses.

We were in the process of moving to his new work location in the south. When he left, the stress of moving sent me back to the hospital for the third and final time. The hospital team dismissed my outside psychologist, as he was responsible for advising me to stop medication after the last two hospitalizations. He came to see me and say good-bye, kissing me on the mouth. I was shocked by his behavior. He seemed happy.

I have stayed on my meds everyday of my life. Until recently, when I developed diabetes insipitus from the long usage of lithium, I faithfully took the lithium each day. I would not trade the help I received from taking lithium for 29 years of my life. The first line of defense against mental illness is taking medicine, and taking it very seriously. Other factors were an aide, but mental illnesses are physical illnesses. The symptoms are not worth the pride often involved in not taking medicine: Tylenol for headaches, psychiatric medicines for mental illnesses. If I had cancer, diabetes, or heart disease that could be stabilized by taking 2+ tablets a day, wouldn't I be thrilled? Yes. However, mental illness has a vicious stigma that must be dealt with before the medication is taken and effective.

My mother-in-law was kind and came for the third time. I was going to ride my bike home, but she forbid it. She was controlling the environment that she could handle and still watch the kids. When I'd come home, she'd tell me to go back to the hospital. The psychologist who led group therapy stated that people in our environment couldn't always handle our need for personal freedom. Looking back, it was not a long wait to go south. I was on meds this time so the CBT skills were much easier to follow.

I said good-bye to the hospital staff on a Friday afternoon. I didn't want to say good-bye to Jan, but I had to do it. Our family went to the Inn where I used to work for the last night. I wore a black dress and we sat downstairs for dinner. I felt dignity and love from my husband and family. He had given up his position and found a new one in the south for the children's sake and mine.

We were on our way to a new world. I had tested well as a mom in the hospital and so had the children. The hospital staff had not recommended the children for therapy. I had known great pain, but had had sufficient strength to discipline myself and raise them. The next day, I cried in the airplane. I was happy that I had tears in my eyes, a sign of emotional health. I saw the skyline of the city. Then I looked at my family, snug inside the plane as we roared into the sky.

CHAPTER EIGHT

New Beginnings (1980-1989)

My family was barely settled in our new house when the phone rang. It was Sister Beatrice, the principal of our children's new Catholic elementary school.

"Hello, dear, I'm following up on an earlier conversation we had regarding our need for a physical education and health teacher. Would you consider the position?" she inquired in a friendly manner. I had just come out of the shower wrapped in a towel to grab the phone. With water drops running down my shoulders, I felt smooth, clean, and dripping with chances to start over.

"Yes, I will accept the position," I said, returning her friendliness.

Bouncing balls greeted my initial efforts as the P.E. teacher. Due to limited space, my office for this new program was in the faculty bathroom. The balls never stayed in the closet but bounced out all over the room and into the toilet. My sense of humor sustained me because the process was nearly driving me into fits of frustration.

I led each class out to the backfields of the school grounds. Warm winds ruffled the pine trees, and the sun was a symbol of God's positive side of life that had eluded me for so long. The children stretched and jumped with their muscles during calisthenics and the games I played with them. I thanked

God for my meds and my psychological support therapy. Happiness was the name of the game that I could finally give to others.

One crisp, beautiful morning I was getting out of my car at the new school annex. I froze as I spotted a man with a rifle in the rearview mirror. He crossed the physical education field and disappeared. I ran inside to tell the teacher, Carol, who was the building supervisor.

"Oh," said Carol, "That's just one of the hunters going to the clay pit to practice shooting for the season."

"How far away from my playing field is the clay pit?" I asked as a mood swing was rising with my level of alarm.

"It's right behind it," was the answer.

With that the guns went off. Then more gunfire continued to punctuate our conversation. I asked if anyone was going to call the police.

"Oh, you can if you wish. We've taken our turn before," the teachers retorted with a noticeable lack of interest.

"I won't take them outside in this gunfire. I will call down to school because someone should take this matter in their hands and stop it. Sister Beatrice should call the police," I fumed, as I could not get an answer at any of the school phone numbers. In desperation I called the rectory where the priest lived. He was most interested in what I had to report.

The children asked me nervously, wanting to know, how come they couldn't go out to play? I gave them a gentle, non-committal answer that would not alarm them, even though they said they could hear the loud noises outside. I taught them the religion lesson I had prepared; it now seemed ironic. At the end of the day I always took Sandra home, the daughter of the chairman of the school board. I was obsessing about how to tell Ellen, her mom, that gunfire was now part of her first grade education. As any responsible mother would be, she was extremely shook-up. So was Denny, her husband.

At the school board meeting two evenings later, Denny presented the gun pit information. It clashed with Sister Beatrice's report that everything was going well at the extension. She admitted to knowing about it and said it would be investigated.

The next day Sister Beatrice was on the warpath. Who had told what about the goings on at the annex? She found out that it was me. In her office, she reprimanded me for not coming to her first. One person in particular was making her life difficult, and on top of that, now I had placed her in a bad light.

I was flabbergasted. For my lack of loyalty, our relationship became diminished and consideration of my needs banished. I had taught P.E., Health, Religion, and Sacred Dance, adding each one to the P.E. as I went along. I resigned at the end of what was my fourth year of teaching on her faculty.

I had developed quite a sense of self-confidence while monitoring the annex problems. I had left a psychiatric unit a few short years ago and yet I was the one who was guarding the children's safety, and yes, OK, their lives. Others seemed blinded by the need for continued employment. I decided to ask two sources of support for their opinion about the gun pit. So, I called my old friend, Dr. Norman Berk.

"Are the children wearing bullet proof vests?" was his only question.

"No," I said, confirming my suspicion that I must be stable as well as valuable in the situation.

Referring to Corinthians, from the Christian scriptures, a passage about people taking turns being the eyes and ears of the community stopped me in my tracks. I was possibly the only eyes and ears at the annex, so I had a significant part to play in the community. The gunfire was an awful way for me to discover that my mental health had increased. Something worthwhile had come out of a nightmare.

The psychologist who conducted the group therapy that I attended each week contacted a priest for me to have spiritual direction. I wanted some spiritual guidance after all the years of psychiatric care. His name was Rev. Fred. The psychologist, Dr. Ann, assured me that I had never met anyone quite like this priest; he was billed as a very holy man and she had known him for a long time.

I met the priest/spiritual director in an old traditional library. As soon as I walked into the room, I threw my long coat and sobbing body on the couch. With my eyes starring up at the ceiling, I opened the conversation,

"I cannot be ordained." Since childhood, I usually kept these longings to myself. My silence in the past helped me to escape the inevitable retort that I had other things in life that were more important. He instantly rejected my admission. He cautiously began speaking while noting that my behavior was not that of someone ready to be a priest, even if I was a female. Self-discipline and self-control were matters of the utmost importance to someone in the religious life.

I calmed down. I had assumed that he would automatically understand the way I felt. I doubted that I would ever transverse the valley between us. Usually I would have controlled myself, but he was supposed to understand, although I didn't really grasp all of the reasons why. Ordination was my by-word for wanting acceptance in the Catholic church as an individual, not placed in the forever-female secondary roles.

He hesitantly agreed to work with me as if it was a marginal decision. He knew Dr. Ann and trusted her decision-making abilities. I felt awkward and beneath him, but I tried to sound honored. I had passed an entrance test to go forward with his type of spiritual direction. He had studied more than other priests and he held advanced degrees.

It might be worthwhile for me to slow down and listen. He had the upper hand and was in his late fifties, too.

He had called me on my overly emotional actions. He did not know much about it yet, but I owned a history from hell when it came to Catholic priests. I had always hoped that someday I would meet the priest who helped me to experience the Northern Lights of peace and the pain of the past would grow dim. Some of my pathology involved my father's death at an early age and my experiences with confession, not so much my mood swings.

I didn't understand that my beautiful eyes, face, and youthful body, might be an obstacle to my spiritual direction. Rev. Fred and I met in the library many times. My husband even went to talk with him and said he had never met anyone that he trusted so implicitly. Rev. Fred came to our home for dinner, assuring us that this was an unusual turn of events for him because he was basically a hermit.

One summer day, I was on my way to a session with Rev. Fred at the library. I gave my jersey top a yank up because good Catholic girls knew we were never to sexually tempt a priest. He was waiting for me in the parking lot and that struck me as odd. He said we were not going to meet in the library. We walked over to a side door of the same building and he opened it for me. I started to have those old feelings that I had come to know as anxiety. I stepped up and turned to the right. All I could see was a bed, and he was following close behind me in the narrow hall. I stopped.

"Go on," he said. I felt trapped. As I entered the bright, cheerful room, I saw an open window. I rushed to jump through it and land on the lawn outside when he came behind me. He slammed the window shut. I turned around and looked at his bedroom. Neat white bookshelves lined one wall, several windows, two comfortable chairs, and the bed. He cordially invited me to relax in the chair in front of the window. Then he picked up the blanket that was folded across his bed.

"My mother gave me this blanket, and I want you to wrap yourself in it because it's chilly in here," he said while standing over my chair and looking down at me.

"NO," I said vehemently. I was becoming emotional in the way that he didn't like. Sometimes he used to say that I was enough to knock someone over. He expressed his hurt and placed the blanket back on his bed.

I planned my strategy: sit tight and agree with anything he had to say that came close to sanity. I did not want to get him aroused or upset. I had a better chance of escaping if I went along with the demeanor that made him comfortable.

"Do you want to go back to the library?" he gently inquired.

" No!" because then I had to get safely past the bed and the blanket, go down the hall, and hope the doors would unlock. He spoke at length about many things for an hour. I was doing well until he said it was time to go. My emotions began to speed and compulsively I said:

"Oh, boy, I cannot wait to get to group therapy today with Dr. Ann and tell everyone what happened this morning!" I said as I lost my cool. I might have done well with a little extra lithium that day. He was very annoyed. He said that this visit to his bedroom had been a compliment. We left and walked out toward the parking lot. He started to walk faster than I did.

"Please tell the good doctor that this was not a rape scene!" he said as he turned back to look at me. The severity of rape had not occurred to me. The sense of shock continued.

I went to group therapy and was glad for the chance to process what life had brought to my doors that day. When I closed my eyes, I saw the jarring and bright lights in my mind that I didn't like. They were present during the group despite the lithium. These lights meant that my emotions were very intense and alarming. I had made only one confrontational statement to Reverend Fred. Dr. Ann was very tense and reiterated that this priest would never harm anyone. She would speak with him.

I always told Richard everything whether or not he really wanted to hear it. He was patient at processing with me. That particular night I felt like I was cooking dinner in the twilight zone. Here I was as the wife and mother I cherished being. I didn't want any more therapy or spiritual direction, church, nuns, or priests for the rest of my life. It's just that they were an intricate part of my world. I taught in a Catholic school, was a DRE in parishes, had a lot of Catholic education, went to the sacraments, and had a Catholic marriage and family life. I eventually understood that I had also attempted to mask mood swings with dysfunctional beliefs concerning religion and authority.

I knew I had to keep processing reality as emotions were coming down in streams. I didn't want to. I wanted to stay at home, but my husband always gently and firmly let me know that I was to continue to face life and grow. I calmed down. Rev. Fred introduced me to a concept taken from Christian spirituality that I grew to master and love: God – me - other. God loves me and wants me to take care of myself so I can love and care for others. If I did not command my own life, I could not interact positively with others. I decided to forgive him. Everyone including my husband and Dr. Ann were surprised but not overly concerned about the whole situation. Apparently my emotions were too strong for everyone's taste.

"He's a man," was the wise wrap-up statement made by Dr. Ann. They were friends, and I thought that many details were avoided in her assessment of his behavior. She summed that it would be a courageous decision if I went back to see him, rather than avoiding him. My grandiosity interlaced with my need to be making independent decisions had already decided to see him. Who was she to be telling me what I already decided? Struggling for my independence was a priority that day.

"You're a beautiful woman," was her other response to the situation. Shocked, I thought I was very plain and not very attractive because I was a former psychiatric patient. What she meant by her two statements never dovetailed for me at that point.

I went to visit him and we sat in the library. He said that he was going on sabbatical. Vague about the reason for his year off, he said that priests took off every few years or so in order to refresh themselves. He believed in the deeper reaches of obedience to his superiors even though he didn't want to go. He was going.

He said that he thought something demonic was involved in inviting me to his bedroom. I silently disagreed. He did apologize and we said a prayer together in the chapel and parted. I was relieved to hear him say that he was going away for at least a year. He recommended I see another priest, Rev. Ben.

Due to the bipolar disorder, emotions took a long time to integrate with the thought process. During the year Rev. Fred was away, some of my wounds were healing. Also, I learned something from Rev. Ben that would benefit my growth in mind, body, and spirit for the rest of my life. A prayer form was to make a considerable difference in my life, as my new spiritual director slowly introduced me to contemplative prayer. We used the traditionally well-known prayer lives of the saints, Teresa of Avila and John of the Cross, as role models.

"The Interior Castle" was a book written by Teresa, an account of her prayer in symbolic form. Inside the castle, the prayer experience moves from one room to another coming closer to union with God, the deepest of prayer experiences. It's a magnificent journey that took me six and one half years to complete the first time. A psychiatrist told me years later she believed that my contemplative prayer life was the main reason for my stability with an unstable disease. In the place of mood swings and subsequent suicidal thoughts, I basked in peace and love. Contemplative prayer gave me a security that I had never had for years.

As I eventually studied spirituality and psychology, I always took note of the relaxing exercises, Christian meditation, and mindfulness exercises. They calm the emotions in the brain processes, strengthening the thought process. They were good material to use myself and with my clients. They enhanced treatment.

The written accounts of prayer during the Reformation are historically the best explanations of contemplative prayer and its behavioral outreach. Rev. Ben was an excellent teacher, but I mostly progressed on my own. I made appointments every six weeks. I did not want to become dependent on a rather well thought, independent, and spiritual man. I strove to do my own work before seeing him.

Teresa of Avila's prayers became a part of me. She was the first person to coin the term mental illness because people commented that some of her nuns did not seem to be right in their mind. She used the term, mental illness, to describe the nuns' problems. She is still acknowledged in psychology textbooks. Praying with her understanding of movement through a castle was all the structure I needed. Peaceful and loving emotions generated within her structure brought me great comfort. The overspill into my daily life with family and work was beyond measure. I've wondered if it was the same for her nuns with their mental illnesses.

It was during this time that I began to see a new psychiatrist, as the older doctor that I saw was retiring. After three or four visits, the new psychiatrist made a valuable observation.

"You do not remind me of someone who is schizophrenic. I think that you are bipolar." I smiled and felt that someone had found the real diagnosis. Bipolar was supposed to be a lighter diagnosis than schizophrenia. Bipolar disorder can take years to diagnose properly. I was now thirty-four, eight years after my first hospitalization at twenty-six.

"I will change your medication and put you on lithium as soon as you trust me," he said.

"I trust you!" was my startling response.

The next session we started to drop the major tranquilizers. I became scared, confused, and a little disoriented. Then he added the lithium two weeks later. I responded well. The world returned to the way I had seen it before my breakdowns. The glaze on my eyesight receded. I was able to think clearly and quickly. I was excited, not ecstatic.

My diagnosis in the hospital had vacillated from acute schizophrenia hysteria upon entrance in the emergency room, to schizophrenia, to schizoaffective, but never bipolar. The DSM Psychiatric Manual determined everyone's hospital diagnoses before 1980. After the new manual in 1980 was in use, I was soon to be diagnosed bipolar 1 disorder. I was so happy with the results of taking lithium daily plus one major tranquilizer tablet a day, that I placed one of my new psychiatrist's appointment cards in my jewelry box. It is still in there with my earrings and necklaces. The medication caused a major change in my level of anxiety and self-confidence.

Eventually I no longer took the one major tranquilizer. I have no reason to go backwards or have false pride about not needing medication. My number one priority is taking my medication. Happily, Teresa of Avila's contemplative prayers, my spiritual director, my new psychiatrist, and my efforts had renewed my world within and without.

I realized that I was coping well with the mental illness beyond my expectations. My family was doing well; I had ended my part time position at school due to the ugly circumstances about the gun-pit.

Each time Richard and I moved for his business promotions, the change of environment was wonderful for my mental health. I had to detach meanings I had accrued to my surroundings and realize there were many options for the way I could view reality. I was beginning to formulate stronger ideas about what I liked and whom I trusted. As a woman who had led her life directed by authoritarian people and organizations in order to deal with her bipolarity, deciding to chart my own course in life was not always a clear or facile process. Moving facilitated the process of claiming myself and stabilizing the bipolarity. I learned that we never live the same day twice.

Our family moves brought me to a new level in my life. I entered a masters degree program to study theology. I maintained a 3.9 cum laude throughout the whole program. The only person who unglued my positive streak was Rev. Fred when he returned from sabbatical.

Reverend Fred taught in the theology program and invited me to take my last course alone in his office. I stayed on my naïve and trusting side and said yes. I felt complimented. As a good Christian, I was ready to forgive the past. However, I picked up a tension between my two spiritual directors, Reverend Fred and Reverend Ben. One was now my teacher and one my spiritual director. Reverend Fred's seeming jealousy translated into wanting to have both positions with me.

In the first session, Reverend Fred told me where to purchase my books for his course. The store was out of the books I needed, but the clerks would order them. I left my name and phone number with the ladies behind the counter. I went on my way to pick up the kids in my carpool at school and drive home. As I entered the kitchen, the phone rang. It was one of the women in the bookstore:

" Reverend Fred has your back up against a wall and we will not sell you any books because he'll trap you. There is nothing we can do for you," the hushed voice reported. Then there was a click and a dead line. I had settled my problems once with Reverend Fred but I still didn't ascribe much credibility to myself in comparison to a priest because I was a former psychiatric patient. He was the well-revered authority figure. The women at the bookstore were known as his friends. Were they jealous of my good fortune, taking a course with him? I was puzzled yet a little scared about their warning. I told Richard and he said to speak about it with Reverend Fred. It is always good to go to the individual first.

After pondering my husband's perspective and praying, I did decide to confront Reverend Fred. When I told him about the phone call, he was very sad. It was his sister's birthday and wondered how anyone could say such things about him? I felt badly for him and went to the other bookstore where he said that I could also find the books.

Reverend Fred began to tell me that he was angry and depressed because his colleagues did not acknowledge his work. He had a paper listing recognized area organizations hanging over his chair. I asked him how come he hung the list? He said it was because his organization where he worked was overlooked and not on the list. Yet he was recently expected to go to the hospital in the middle of the night to help a woman who was raped.

As the course with Reverend Fred continued, I was strong academically but still growing emotionally. My emotions were aligning nicely with my thought process through my psychiatric medicine, psychotherapy, and education. I was receiving all A's as testimony of how well I was doing. Around him my emotions could wash over my thinking, and a back and forth struggle would happen inside me. Sometimes Reverend Fred talked about the third way; higher authorities among the priests sanctioned this practice. Authority still held sway in my discernment processes. He taught me that the third way was a way that a priest could be affectionate with a student, and it would not affect my grade. I mused about whose authority operates in any given situation: my authority or the religious person's authority, a Catholic priest?

He kissed me occasionally. Years later I wondered if my weak perceptions didn't discern a seduction process. I had just left group therapy at the psychologist's suggestion because I was doing so well. I was denying that maybe I was not strong enough to handle the anxieties this man was creating in my life.

Looking back is always easier, but I wish I had gone to my psychologist, Dr. Ann, for an individual session, even if she didn't support my perceptions. I think my pride got in the way as she had released me from group, and I felt honored. I was doing well with family life, school, and friendships. I now know that I was not handling more stressful situations as well as I thought that I was. Denial stopped my ability to assess what he was doing. I obsessively reminded myself that I was the former psychiatric patient and he the impressive priest and professor. Dr. Ann had said that he wouldn't harm me. Richard had told me to speak directly to him and I had. Nonetheless, I was mounting enormous emotional stress and ambivalence during my studies with Reverend Fred.

He was well aware of my psychiatric/hospitalization background of a few years ago from Dr. Ann's referral. I knew that I would take lithium for life even though I had left group therapy at this point. However, Dr. Ann had not supported me in the past incident when Rev. Fred took me to his bedroom. She toed a neutral position. I knew that he was admired in the church and town community. Slowly I began to become more isolated from others and from my own thought process. He knew my past but also expected me to hold my own in his course. He was still the authority figure like a string of authority father figures since my daddy died. I was struggling to replace them all with my own authority.

One day after a lesson, I stood up to say goodbye to Reverend Fred. Everything moved fast. What happened that day is called sexual assault. I immediately denied to myself what had just happened, and thus I never spoke to anyone about the situation at the time.

According to Wikipedia, rape in criminal law is an assault by a person involving sexual intercourse without that person's consent. However, outside the law the term is often used interchangeably with sexual assault, a closely related form of assault to rape. Sexual assault is an assault of a sexual nature on another personal. Health and emotional problems can be the long-term results.

Sexual assault is what happened to me that day in Reverend Fred's office.

In the months ahead, my memory ebbed and flowed about what had transpired. I was not strong enough to face the situation or think of professionals in the community who would even be supportive of my problem. At the end of the children's school year, Richard and I were preparing to move up north again. Moving is a stressful time and I don't remember thinking about the incident or telling Richard. I didn't feel guilty but sexually abused women follow a pattern of repressing and denying the material for years. That's a reason the sexual abuse commissions of later years in the Catholic church extended the statue of limitations. The human mind will not remember until it feels safe. In addition, three weeks later I was diagnosed with rheumatoid arthritis. The arthritis pain consumed most of my daily activities, making it even harder to reflect and remember the emotional connection.

When the course was over, I went to Reverend Fred's office expecting an apology like once before in the library. I sat down; I was alarmed when he took out a penknife, looking angry. I reacted with a fearful face.

"You have chewing gum on the bottom of your shoe," he stated, as he dragged my foot onto his lap, scraping off the gum.

"You see, we each have a different version of what the knife is for – you were frightened but I was not," he continued.

"Furthermore, the last visit was no rescuer and no rescue," he said emphatically. Sometimes around him I was in command of myself and then suddenly I would not be in command. Mood swings were causing a strong dissonance. This time I thought that the conversation lend itself to a quick exit. He did not assault me again. At graduation a few weeks later, my fears mounted again when he kissed me on the mouth in front of everyone. He did so with an angry, sexual look on his face.

Our family moved when Richard's company assigned him to a new position. We moved with heavy hearts. Once again a new life needed to be created out of the fabric of our family's reservoir of strength. The teenagers were very upset. We tried to explain that their dad's career promotion once again required a move. Yes, it was far away from their friends. They could go back to visit. Their friends could come to visit us in our new home.

CHAPTER NINE
Integration (1989-2012).

After the move, I went to see my new psychiatrist, Dr. Stan, and said that I only wanted medication appointments, not psychotherapy. My psychiatric medicine along with my contemplative prayer life stabilized me for work and school. The prayer, in particular, brought an evenness and peace that spilled into my new endeavors. Following this course of action for a year or so was working out well. One exception was the off and on flashbacks to the scene with Reverend Fred.

I finally stopped the denial process and faced the brokenness of the sexual assault two years or so after we had settled in our new home. I made an appointment to see Dr. Stan. He sounded curious and a little frustrated.

" I thought you were only coming for medication maintenance," he said, looking at me over his appointment book. I explained that I was surprised myself. He agreed to see me for psychotherapy as well as medication.

Dr. Stan addressed the worst of the anxiety that still felt wrapped around my body, and I began the process of letting go of the pain, humiliation, the entire situation, and the aftermath of the sexual assault. Re-building respect for my own sexuality, going out into life to practice protecting myself from danger, and learning again how to enjoy the presence of men with self-control was arduous. Therapy for one sexual assault: two and one half years.

I worked hard with Dr. Stan to decide how I would take care of myself in the aftermath of the sexual assault. In the end I decided to ask for an informal investigation into the sexual assault at the institute of higher learning where it occurred. I did it to help Reverend Fred as well as the community and myself.

I didn't know about the Catholic commissions that were conducting investigations concerning priests who were charged with sexual allegations. Many people after me sued, but I wanted reconciliation, not money. I now know Christianity moves slower than the courts. My approach was a part of my spirituality that I wanted to keep. God loves me, so I embrace the love for myself, and that enables me to love others. I was also protecting my mending mind from a grueling court session. I decided that the informal investigation met all of my needs for compassion for all of us involved in the situation. As a result of the investigation, Reverend Fred was given several years of psychotherapy. I had stood up for myself and yet I was sad that I never heard the word, sorry, from anyone at the institution, including the head of the investigation, Reverend Ben.

Telling my husband was another significant part of the healing process. When I told him, he shook with anger. I remember his eyes popping out with fury. However, I was able to tell him that I was taking care of myself and that I had contacted the institution in order to have the informal investigation. I didn't want to sue, I wanted reconciliation in all forms possible. Richard calmed down. He always wanted me to be a professional woman. I had taken a serious blow in a professional environment. I came back and took care of myself. I didn't fail. That fact was the most important component to Richard. Also, I told him in a composed manner. I didn't throw myself at him as if I were a little girl who was scared to death. As always, self-care was my best answer for all concerned.

I had applied to the diocesan offices in our new home to be a Director of Religious Education. I was assigned to a parish that was an hour and fifteen minutes away from my new home. I planned my days and nights of work according to the teenagers' schedules at home. My contract stated that I was to pull together the needs of five parishes. Many of the parish services usually provided were lost over the last several years. Also, I was voted by the other Directors of Religious Education (DRE's) to become a member of the DRE Board of advisors for the archdiocese in the city.

My mind was working very well. I had lots of reading and planning to do. I was really happy that first autumn. I had purchased a ceramic vase and put wispy blue flowers in it to go in front of a Blessed Mother's statue on my office windowsill. I could feel that I was doing something worthwhile for these communities. I did have trouble holding my pen or pencil because my hands were swelling from the rheumatoid arthritis inflammation. I would stick the pen between my thumb and middle finger and write away. I paid next to no attention to the fact that my hands were getting worse. I paid a lot of attention to my work and my thankfulness that I could work. I uttered small prayers to myself as I went along through my days. Swells of peace and joy were pointing to a healthy self-concept.

I still remember the snow falling down lightly against the bricks of the wall outside my window. I was the happiest person alive. I was also being paid to plan and work with the knowledge I had acquired in the theology degree. I loved it. My school studies and DRE fit like kid gloves. Having a bipolar diagnosis appeared to have passed away even though I knew it had not.

From my point of view, I still had developmental lags. I still didn't know how to handle different situations. I was missing an outer shell to let things roll off my back. They seemed to stick to me. Working in the church as a layperson, I accepted the occurrence of the clergy's ostracism and the nun's ambivalence. Every time I wanted to leave my DRE position or the Catholic church, someone would tell me to be patient. The nuns and priest were often authoritarian in their approach to lay professionals. The winds of change would come and the laity would be respected. However, I was nowhere near finished with my negative encounters with church officials.

Polarized

I do not blame the entire Catholic church because I was sexually abused and harassed by Catholic priests. Although I can no longer be a member due to resulting health reasons, my hopes, dreams, and prayers are still that the church as a whole finds the freedom that Jesus Christ intended for his church. I image a church where power belongs to God, given to us to fuel our gifts and talents. The only power worthy of his church is the power of love. It can only be achieved at this point through the reconciliation that I pray will happen, somewhere in a dawn.

Silently, I called myself an idealistic parish mystic. I supported the lay volunteer women who worked in the parish programs. Being left out by my religious colleagues was painful, but in my mind, I had a calling and a mission. I also wondered if I was strong enough to leave my job. I started looking around for another position closer to home. I was having success at the archdiocesan level. Nonetheless, I decided to go to another diocese where everything was supposedly more up to date.

As a DRE in the next parish, birthdays were times for the staff to celebrate together. Flowers and cakes were prepared for each nun and some token for the priests. At the October staff meeting the newest priest announced that he was holding a B-B-Q roast pig behind the rectory for the priests and nuns. The date was the night of my birthday. Being the only lay staff member, I put two and two together that I was probably being roasted in effigy as a pig. I stayed home for a day or two.

I can still remember that the same priest would not allow me in church on the night of the sacrament of reconciliation for the children. It was my responsibility to prepare them for the sacrament. His attitude toward me started when we shared the podium for an adult reconciliation workshop. He spoke forty-five minutes over his time. I finally stood up and quietly told him that he had to stop. He did but I never heard the end of his angry arrogance. He was eventually listed as a pedophile and dismissed from the priesthood, but not before he was promoted to pastor for another parish.

I resigned. I give myself lots of credit for pulling out of destructive situations. I also credit ongoing therapy with Dr. Stan. I had plenty of examples for him of interactions with men besides Richard. I had had enough. Dr. Stan retorted with the punt that I would never be able to stop self-care in regard to sexual interactions. I shot him a look of amazed fright.

I studied in a master's program for pastoral counseling. I could go to see Dr. Stan as often as needed. One to four times a month I would process how I was taking care of myself in arenas that were first and foremost very real. I was learning to accept my own humanity.

At the end of the counseling classes for the M.A. program, students did an internship. It was up to me to find a 300-400 hour therapeutic supervised setting with a professional counselor. I found my place in a hospital outpatient clinic for seriously ill patients; most were relatively poor. The M.S. clinician asked me to do 800 hours like the other internists who were Ph.D. level students. He had never accepted a M.A. student before me. The fact that I was a pastoral counselor was intriguing to him. It would be interesting to see what a difference my interdisciplinary approach would bring to the clients.

Between my studies and family life, I used up all of my energy. I remember the pain of rheumatoid arthritis. I know it was a constant cross in my life because there was no medicine until methatrexate was introduced in the mid-1990's to ease the pain in all of my joints and muscles. I exercised as much as possible.

I never saw myself as better than the Ph.D. students. In fact, I cringed at the slightest criticism, taking it to heart. It was a pain as searing as my rheumatoid arthritis. I did silently take credit for staying and actually finishing a doctoral level internship, actually the only internist who finished the 800 hours that year. Nonetheless, any mistakes caused me to implore the Almighty to strengthen me in my cherished disciple. Our supervisor reinforced the horror of forgetting certain questions in the intake. It was more than a mistake to forget to ask the client if he or she were suicidal or homicidal. We would have to stay late, sometimes until 8:00 p.m. for forgetting to ask these questions.

"You have allowed a sick person to go back on the streets, the highways and byways of life without the proper care," he would lecture us. It didn't take long to remember. Our offices were on the second floor. A guard was always waiting at the bottom of the elevator ride to escort each of us to our cars. If it was after hours, the guard was not on duty. It could be a dangerous walk to our cars; it could be as dangerous as someone left out in the cold feeling suicidal or homicidal. We never forgot.

A professor in the master of pastoral counseling program taught one of the last classes. It was on sexuality. With each week it moved from the sublime to the absurd. The woman sitting next to me stopped showing up. We were told that she had committed suicide. She had a multiple personality disorder. At that time, no one could be forced into private therapy. Actually, I don't know how anyone could be forced. Nobody forced me and I wanted to go. I was overly particular about taking care of my own mind.

The professor/priest for the course was teaching folks in the 40 to 60 years-old ranges. However, he put the correct missionary position on the chalkboard for us to grasp the best possible position for a woman to reach orgasm. He walked around the room bending down in front of various women.

"If I took you in the other room and took off your blouse, I could fondle you." It would not really be sex because it isn't intercourse," he would tell us with great authority. He came to my desk twice during the course material.

"You are so beautiful, Patricia, that I will go home and masturbate," he said in a loud voice, throwing his arms up to the ceiling. One day I ran into his office with some paperwork for him to sign. Quickly he signed the papers and put his pen down. He strode to the front door of his office and threw his arms across the door. I smiled and waited for what seemed like a small eternity. He put his arms down and let me out.

It was the last course of the entire program. Nobody wanted to flunk out at that point, but we all complained to the other professors about his behavior. They were appalled and told us that he had to stop bringing his pathology into the classroom. When authority figures are told about what is going on in a classroom that should be enough to correct his behavior. He did quiet down.

When it came time for the oral examination to complete the master's program, he was the one of two professors on my committee. He refused to pass me, saying that I didn't handle my sexuality very well. The other professors were angry at his usual antics.

A team of five professors and my intern supervisor in the field had to pass on my work. My supervisor in the field told me he wrote some comments to the effect that this professor was having some problems that affected his approach to me. They passed me. I left. I didn't go to graduation.

Graduating was an honor; I wanted to let someone know about my bipolar disorder. Dr. Stan said to wait until someone asked me if I was crazy. Nobody volunteers his/her ailments, and I was not to think that I was unusual in this regard. I knew that there was a stigma. To this day, nobody has ever asked.

After school ended, I was very reticent to start a position as a psychotherapist. Even though my therapeutic skills were shown in class as exemplary, I knew where I had come from psychiatrically. I wanted to bring the best of my experiences and successes to bear on my counseling with other people.

I knew Dr. Stan was not very happy with my decision to wait while I made sure I felt ready to take what I thought of as a serious plunge. Nobody can service all the diagnoses. I decided then, and again in the Ph.D. program, consulting doctors and professors, to not treat bipolar clients. It takes tremendous objectivity to treat your own kind, especially a severe disorder. In limiting myself, I happily treated many clients of other populations.

Polarized

I had weaknesses and strengths. I needed to think about myself beyond what school and ongoing therapy could afford me. I was going to be the best therapist for my clients that I could. School had seemed to me to be only a part of my preparation. My own therapy of almost twenty years was the other part. I wanted to integrate those two parts before I went forward in a very serious and responsible manner. So, against everyone else's better judgment, I took a year to integrate before I applied for positions like my fellow students did after graduation. I grew in self-definition. At year's end, I saw an ad in a local newspaper for a position as a therapist in a private clinic. I went for an interview and accepted the position. It mainly served Medicaid clients. As a pastoral counselor I wanted to start with the poor, so I started working soon after the interview. It was 1992, fifteen years after I had left the hospitalizations behind.

I had prepared to begin my career as a counselor. I had unearthed and addressed enough of my pathological father and priest patterns to feel free. No one is completely healed in this life. However, remnants of remembered pain can keep us open to empathic and compassionate responses to others. I continued in my habit of contemplative prayer and of healing my own wounds, too.

I prayed for one hour each day, deep in peace and love. It continued as one of the tools that stabilized me across my life. Moreover, I could never cease thanking God for making my life reasonable. I was thankful for my family life, too. Now my work made it even more important to take the time for prayer and reflection every afternoon.

I felt peaceful with each client I saw in the clinic; I had a rather spiritual perspective of each person that I never verbalized to the client. It was just the starting point for forming a relationship with each person. I could see the two of us changed when the client's blocks he/she brought to therapy were removed. We worked on treatment plans. I had that unspoken confidence that the client would grow personally and reach his/her goals. Thus, I non-verbally motivated the clients who came to see me. I saw children, teenagers, adults, and couples with a variety of problems. I had put myself through all sorts of therapy, education, and personal exploration. No one can do that in a few months when it took me fifteen years. The clients moved at their own pace. Some were healthier than I ever was. I was aware of my strengths that were excellent, but I had also learned that those same strengths could boomerang into weaknesses if I relinquished my own efforts at self-care.

As far as I am concerned, being a therapist means constant growth. It means real effort on my part personally. I am the only instrument in the room with the client. No machines can create a relationship that so many people have lacked in their lives. If one client had a good experience with me and understood that there are genuinely positive relationships in this world, I accomplished a great deal. I saw many clients grow and leave with self-care in operation. I received compliments on my work from the director and several people thought that I should pursue a Ph.D.

Dr. Stan was one of those people who were after me to apply to a Ph.D. program. He said it didn't matter to him what program I applied to as long as it was a Ph.D. program. He said that such a doctoral program would strengthen my cognitions. He added that I was bright enough to handle a Ph.D. He wouldn't let me off the hook.

My husband agreed,

"Trisha, you really are a doctor. You are bright, articulate, and you have pressured yourself endlessly to pull yourself together. You have worked harder than most to get where you are today, and the family has benefited from your efforts," he said. Both of them knew my need for a push when it came to something that I thought was out of my self-concept zone.

Okay, I'd apply. I was secretly pleased to be getting their support because I thought I might like it. So I applied to a few programs. I sabotaged one interview, as I was pretty sure that I wanted to go to another school. The sabotaged school put me on their waiting list and I wasn't surprised. It was a secular school and was probably the most sensible choice.

However, the one I wanted came from a combination of factors. I likened it to a piece of twisted Christmas candy. Red is for faith and courage; white for forgiveness and forgetting; and green for the forever green of going back. (It is the green that is the stumbling block of abused people). I had to go to a school where I could make it clear to the whole world that I had faith in my maker. Collaboration with God had brought me to this juncture in my life. There was no force on the face of this earth that would allow me to accept the honor of starting a Ph.D. program without acknowledging my God.

I had a good interview at the school of my choice with the director of clinical education. He eventually became the chair of my dissertation committee. During the summer, I received my acceptance letter from the Pastoral Counseling Ph.D. Program at Loyola University Maryland. Pastoral Counseling is an interdisciplinary degree. It is the interface between theology and mental health counseling. Most ventures in life are interdisciplinary and complex. I found it to be a dynamic perspective. My mind worked very hard and was able to handle more complex material. This experience enriched the rest of my life.

During the same summer, Richard's world of work ended. His company's board of directors brought in a CEO who dismantled the entire company. The stocks soared, and a few made profits at the expense of many. Fortunately, a company wanted to hire him in the south. I was frantic. I had moved so many times for my husband's work that I was really upset this time. I had something I really wanted in life besides psychiatric and psychological sessions to work on my work.

Richard stated that he wanted me to go to this school anyway. I had moved so many times for the family that he wanted me to have this degree as a present. It would be my empty nest syndrome as the kids were also going off to college.

"Fly up here in a plane. Stay with classmates. Do whatever you need to do to start the degree," he said.

"It is valuable and vital to your future well-being." He could not be more emphatic about what he thought.

Richard and I moved south. I climbed over all of the unpacked boxes in our new home to get into the garage and drive myself to the airport. I got settled in a classmates' abode and went over to registration. The pain in my arms and legs was exquisite. There was nothing to kill the arthritic pain. I always thought of it as a buffer from the world. It provided the objectivity that I had always needed. My major professor smiled that I had flown back to go to the program. I smiled, too, but for different reasons.

From the start I was there to develop myself as a role model and professional member of my mental health population. Psychiatrists told me that I had to work at least 5 years past the Ph.D. to be considered an excellent role model to the professional community. With extreme rheumatoid arthritis pain in my arms and legs, I quickly signed the registration papers. I felt manic energy flowing through me as a positive force for grasping the pen and setting my goals. Eight and a half years later, I was informed that I could graduate. It was spring of 2003.

My swollen hands from the rheumatoid arthritis drew attention those school years and frankly made my student life difficult. The last few years were easier as methatrexate was on the market for pain. I stayed home to write my dissertation. *The Incremental Validity of Religious Problem-Solving Styles, Images of God, and Image of the Holy Spirit as Predictors of Emotional Distress* was my dissertation title and the cognitive learning tool Dr. Stan must have had in mind. The dissertation was a discipline that I never encounter before or after. Complexity of life never eluded me again.

I turned down the hard earned right to go to graduation. One of the professors sent me a diploma and a description of graduation. I would have walked across the stage in front of thousands of people, been hooded - the colors of my degree on an academic hood placed over my head - and then I would have walked over to accept my diploma while everyone cheered and clapped. My family and friends could come but not the second mental health family I respected since I was twenty-six. I had to practice for five years before I could acknowledge them.

There was also the matter of the mentally ill who were as smart as me but maybe without some of the resources I had. What if they wanted to study for a Ph.D. or follow another dream? On the positive side of being bipolar, we are known for our genius, gifts, and talents. My contribution may have started as small as a mustard seed, but I have the self-confidence that it is very valuable. I always thought I put my resources to the best use that I could for my population, but I'm only one person. I find comfort in reading the efforts of so many in the field of mental health. Still I could not bring myself to walk across the stage as if I hadn't had unusual support to accomplish an extraordinary feat.

A Ph.D. is the highest academic award anyone can achieve. When graduation was over, Dr. Stan said his guess was that there are only approximately 2,000 Ph.D.'s or M.D.'s in the world at any given time that were diagnosed bipolar before, during, or after an M.D. or Ph.D. education. I want to go to graduation when today's children have access to a cure. I want the children to be free of mental illness to become whoever they conceive themselves to be. I could not go to graduation because I'm waiting for the children to cross the stage with me.

I worked for sixteen years total as a pastoral counselor and a Licensed Professional Counselor (LPC), including six years beyond the Ph.D. I developed and was director of a Pastoral Counseling Center in a hospital setting. Earlier I established a parish ministry, and I did an externship in the Employee Assistance Program at Duke University Medical Center. I was also the counselor for a homeless shelter. I worked with high-end professionals as well as working class folks. I loved every minute of it. I received my Fellowship in Addictions Recovery, not out of my own need, but to understand the addicted population more thoroughly. The Fellowship covered treatments based on the Alcoholics Anonymous 12 Step Program and research and skills from the field of Mental Health. The interdisciplinary approach enlarged and enhanced both disciplines in a creative manner.

My present day psychiatrist believes that I couldn't see what was transpiring in situations with the priests or cope with the dangers in order to remain healthy. The damage from the sexual assault had left a deep mark that I could not seem to erase. When Richard and I left the Catholic church, my experience of God's love and new direction came as a surprise. Gone were the days of guilt and false humility. I had found a new place under the sun. It did not have a manic quality; moreover, I had a mild happiness that I had searched for most of my life. I moved along trusting God all the way. The members of the Survivors Network of those Abused by Priests (SNAP), reported the same type of positive experiences upon leaving the church, although I am not a member. They speak of new paths in society that are led by God. Furthermore, my psychiatrist noted that I was in contact with my siblings, an unusual occurrence for people with bipolar disorder. Families are often alienated and sometimes each other's locations are not known. God had led me home to myself and loved ones were still in my life.

I can now speak up that I am a doctor and a human being who has, at this point, a mild form of bipolarity. I am not cured because there is no cure for me, for others, or most sadly the children who often do not know why they feel so poorly. Ongoing research is necessary. The pathophysiology of bipolar disorder is not completely understood, and the causality of bipolar disorder is not fully determined. Many interacting components may someday fit together to give us a better picture of the disorder. The thyroid gland and bipolar research have found groundbreaking connections that bring hope. Brain research is progressing and reducing the mystery associated with bipolar disorder.

All together I worked for sixteen years as a pastoral counselor. I pushed myself despite rheumatoid arthritis and bipolar 1 disorder to meet my goals. My body finally signaled me that I had pushed hard enough. I didn't take the year off after the Ph.D. like other students did to rest and recuperate. I had a dream to pursue immediately. I wanted to share my life if it helped others suffering from mental illness. I took my medicine everyday and that was a large part of my success. I figured out that I needed a clear mind to work with a strong spirit and a cooperative body, if not a perfectly healthy body. Memories drove me on days when I wanted to give up. Dreaming was part of my human experience. Making dreams come true takes effort, sacrifice, collaboration, and prayer.

I flew into La Guardia Airport in New York. I hopped a cab and told the driver to please take me to the Empire State Building. I paid and walked into the building. I went up the elevator to the observation deck. I walked across the platform and grabbed onto the black curved wrought iron bars. As I was gazing down into the lake in Central Park, I felt little fingers wiggling under my hands. I untangled our entwined fingers and saw a charm bracelet on her wrist. She turned and leaned against my side. Holding hands, we stole a look at each other and smiled. We walked over to the elevator and together we pushed the down button.

Made in the USA
Charleston, SC
14 August 2013